reveals a healing path as ageless as it is unconventional. There will be many who will find comfort in these pages."

—PAUL SIBCY, author of *Healing Your Rift With God: A Guide to Spiritual Renewal and Ultimate Healing*

"Rev. Jerry Bongard's work as a spiritual counselor is pioneering and extraordinarily valuable for science and society alike. The term "near birth experience" will soon be widely known and used, with great acclaim. It identifies a new psychotherapeutic means by which people can consciously contact their own soul or spirit-center for healing, wisdom and love. Unlike the near death experience, which likewise profoundly alters a person's manner of living, the near birth experience can be voluntarily accessed and does not require a person to nearly die. It demonstrates the reality of existence before and after this life; it also demonstrates the eternal presence of the divine and its intelligent design for our lives."

—JOHN WHITE, author of *The Meeting of Science and Spirit*

"*The Near Birth Experience* gives us a clear glimpse of our divine nature. It is a must-read for everyone on a spiritual path."

—DHARMA SINGH KHALSA, M.D., author of *Brain Longevity*, *The Pain Cure*, and *Meditation as Medicine*.

THE
NEAR BIRTH
EXPERIENCE

JERRY BONGARD

THE NEAR BIRTH EXPERIENCE

A Journey to the Center of Self

FOREWORD BY HAL ZINA BENNETT, PH.D.

MARLOWE & COMPANY
NEW YORK

Published by
Marlowe & Company
A Division of the Avalon Publishing Group Incorporated
841 Broadway
New York, NY 10003
The Near Birth Experience: *A Journey to the Center of Self*
Copyright © 2000 by Jerry Bongard
Foreword copyright © 2000 by Hal Zina Bennett

The poem "I Know Them," is reprinted on p. 77
by kind permission of the author.

Library of Congress Cataloging-in-Publication Data
Bongard, Jerry.
The near birth experience: a journey to the center of self/ Jerry Bongard; foreward by Hal Zina Bennett.
p. cm.
Includes bibliographical references.
ISBN 1-56924-602-5
1. Hypnotic age regression. 2. Pre-existence. 3. Spiritual life—Miscellanea. I. Title

BF1156.R45B66 2000
133.9'01'35—dc21   00-56217

9 8 7 6 5 4 3 2 1

DESIGNED BY KATHLEEN LAKE, NEUWIRTH AND ASSOCIATES, INC.

Distributed by Publishers Group West
Printed in the United States of America

To my wife Gail,

who chose to spend her adult life with me,

often putting up with the difficulties of a committed relationship,

and to Laurie, Mary, and Julie

who chose us as their parents.

Each of these four women has loved me at my best and at my worst, and has taught me the meaning of family. Each in her own way has confirmed for me the central message of the near birth experience—that we are all meant for joy, and love is the path. I do not know how to express my gratitude to them, but I hope they can glimpse it as they read between the lines of my behavior.

CONTENTS

CONTENTS

FOREWORD

by Hal Zina Bennett

E very now and then a new author comes along with a perspective that forces us to pause and take a closer look at the values and beliefs we take for granted. When Jerry Bongard's manuscript came to me in the mail two years ago, I was literally stopped in my tracks. I knew about near death experiences. I'd had one myself that literally changed my life. But near birth? What could that be about?

As I sat down to read the manuscript I was reminded of a story my friend Jerry Jampolsky tells in his lectures and books. Friends of his had a new baby in their house and on the baby's first day home their four-year-old daughter crept into the baby's room and asked,

"Baby, can you tell me about God? I'm starting to forget."

Here, it seemed to me, was at least anecdotal evidence for the possibility that we do bring into this lifetime memories that belong to a time and space prior to our births. What's more, those pre-birth experiences have an impact on our lives that are at least as important as what kinds of parenting we receive in our first five years as sentient beings on this planet.

Jerry's and his clients' stories about their near birth experiences and the epiphanies surrounding them are as convincing as they are dramatic. While I have always been convinced that we do not come into life empty-handed, I had never even imagined that there was a way to recall memories of life in the womb, much less prior to our conception. And if Jerry has not given me scientific proof that these memories are real, he at least convinces me, beyond a shadow of a doubt, that looking for answers in the near birth experience can unlock secrets about the meaning of our lives that are indeed profound.

Courageous pioneers of the human psyche are slowly peeling away the thin membrane that separates the invisible world of spirit from the everyday world of the material realities that so dominate our attention. Certainly Pastor Bongard must be counted among that hardy group of spiritual teachers who are leading us deeper into the world of spirit and personal meaning.

As we move toward more spiritual or transpersonal tools for exploring our own identities, it is becoming clearer and clearer that we can no longer ignore our spiritual relationships to a power greater than ourselves. We find our true meaning and purpose not by searching through psychology textbooks or even religious tracts. These may prove to be little more than helpful, if limited, tools for self-exploration. To go further, we need to turn our focus inward in new ways, and the near birth experience is, I believe, an important tool for doing this.

Pioneers like Jerry Bongard are forging an important path that can carry us beyond pathologizing the human condition. Modern psychology, starting with Freud, began applying the pathology model to the eternal quest for meaning and purpose about a hundred years ago. So it is a pretty new idea if seen within the perspective of a few million years of evolution. While this pathology model has served us well in some regards, it has set off three generations of questers who have made a lifetime career of peeling the onion of their own psyches. Too often that quest has taken them further from life, not closer to it, providing little more than a new and complicated illusion of separation and aloneness.

Bongard is among a very different group of questers who are finding answers not by looking at what is wrong with our lives, but by looking for what's right. The real contribution of the near birth experience concept, I believe, is that it offers us a tool for finding that place where we first experienced our spiritual Source. By reliving such experiences and bringing them into our present lives, we open up to a brand new way of looking at ourselves and our relationships to the cosmos in which we are immersed.

In reading this book I could not help but go back to my own

pre-birth memories. I remember, at the age of four or five, recalling something that had come before my birth. I tried to explain to my parents that I had such memories but at that age I did not have the words to communicate what I was feeling, nor did my parents have the understanding to explore these feelings with me. In the process of reading this book I at last recalled not specific images but a sensation of infinite space and infinite love, a space without form or time. It was and is a wonderful experience and I now draw upon that memory whenever I get caught up in the busyness of everyday life. These memories remind me of the real meaning and purpose of our lives, as spiritual beings trying to come to terms with this finite form which we have momentarily been given.

I would hope that readers of this book might get as much as I have from this work. The author's concepts, stories and modest tools can help us travel the path toward our original connection with Spirit. And out of that can come a new understanding of our relationships with ourselves, each other, and Creation itself.

—Hal Zina Bennett, M.S., Ph.D., is the author of thirty books, including *Spirit Circle*, a visionary novel, and *Write from the Heart: Unleashing the Power of Your Creativity*. His newest book is *Animal Spirits and the Wheel of Life* (Hampton Roads Publishers, 2000).

Acknowledgments
and Thanks

To Gail: for your love, your support, and for creating a family with such enthusiasm for the things of the spirit. You are the eternal treasure of my life. Thanks for putting up with me during the many, often frustrating hours when I was writing this manuscript.

To Laurie, Mary, and Julie: You have been a renewing source of joy for me since before you were even born, and each of you has contributed to my life and to this book in ways that are invaluable. I love each of you more than you can know.

To Steve, Todd, Dave, Justin, Aaron, Nicole, and Kyle: I am so glad you are part of my life and my family. I look forward always to the times we are together, for you also help me remember the meaning of life as it is connected to love.

To Mom and Dad: for giving me the certainty that God is.

To those who have allowed me to share in your near birth experiences: Thanks for your trust.

To the Board of Chrysalis Counseling Center—Norm Petersen, Bill Grace, Diane Lewis, Thad Mills, Tom Sconzo, and Larry Severance—thanks for your encouragement. For Jeanne Mace, a special thanks for your support. Aerial Long, you were there to help me meet with the Light. Thank you.

To Jamal Rahman, for your help, friendship, and the Sufi stories.

To John White for the years of support he gave encouragement, telling me that this manuscript was of value and should be published.

To Cindy Grochowski, for your suggestions for the manuscript.

To Hal Zina Bennett and Susan Sparrow for your help in getting this book published, thank you, thank you. You were invaluable at the time I most needed help. Hal, your foreword and editing have made all the difference!

INDNJC

Our birth is but a sleep and a forgetting:
The Soul that rises with us, our life's Star,
Hath had elsewhere its setting,
And cometh from afar:
Not in entire forgetfulness,
And not in utter nakedness,
But trailing clouds of glory do we come
From God, who is our home:
Heaven lies about us in our infancy!
Shades of the prison-house begin to close
Upon the growing Boy,
But he beholds the light, and whence it flows,
He sees it in his joy;

—Ode: Intimations of Immortality
from Recollections of Early Childhood
by William Wordsworth[1]

THE
NEAR BIRTH
EXPERIENCE

❋

Introduction

When my grandson Aaron was three, he thought I was magic. I could take a quarter or any small object, put it in my hand, put my hands behind my back and say, "Abra cadabra, alaca zam! Disappear!" Then I'd show him my empty hand. "Grandpa, you disappeared it!" he would exclaim. Then I would put my hand behind my back again, say the magic words, and Presto! There it was! "You appeared it again!" he would say. He was amazed every time. Then he would try it, taking the coin and saying the magic words, and be disappointed that it hadn't disappeared. For quite some time he did not know that I had hidden the object in my back pocket and then retrieved it.

He was convinced that I was magic, and he knew that someday he would be able to do it too, if only he said the magic words right, or knew the secret. He was right, of course. Now he can do it. Now he knows the process that can bring the same "magic" results.

In the same way, the process for regressing to the womb may seem like magic to those who first experience it. And for many people the results are amazing. But it isn't magic. Almost anyone can learn to retrieve these memories when they try the process I describe here. In my experience, about nine out of ten people who try it are successful in going back as far as the womb. Of these, about half are able to go back to the beginning of life, even before they entered the womb, to remember their life purpose and a time when they were in communion with a Being of Light, a time when they knew, really knew, that they were then, and always would be, essentially good.

The near birth experience is similar to various techniques of "rebirthing" in that it helps a person remember or relive the experience of the baby in the womb. These two procedures differ in many ways, however. The communion shared with a Higher Power, or Being of Light, is undoubtedly the most significant difference, for in the near birth experience we go back to a time even before our conception. Rebirthing can provide us with important insights about our relationships with our mothers and with our first experience of separating from her body and becoming a separate being. The near birth experience does that too, but in addition the near birth experience provides us with insights that confirm for us our relationship with the spiritual Source from which all life springs.

For some people, the idea of remembering a time in the womb, or remembering a time even before that, is hard to believe. For this reason, many professionals have been reluctant to write about such things, afraid they will lose credibility among their peers. In his book *Hypnosis: The Application of Ideomotor Techniques*, Dr. Cheek, whose work inspired my own, writes:

> Some of the ideas presented here, such as considering the perceptions and understandings of the infant at birth, were being explored during our workshops and our private practice . . . I felt, however, that we should refrain from writing about these matters until their therapeutic value had been established by other observers.

Then Dr. Cheek adds, "I believe this time has come."[1]

Dr. Cheek wrote this in 1994. I agree with him. The time has come to share this information, and that is the reason I have written this book. Yet it is easy to understand why many professionals who have worked with this material are reluctant even now to share information regarding a conscious life in the womb, much less reports of life before entering the womb. They may fear that they will meet with a skeptical audience or that their professional credibility will be questioned. They might even be labeled as a "kook."

When Dr. Dabney Erwin first encountered the process of age regression, which is part of the near birth experience, he wrote: "My first reaction to this was more than disbelief; it was a judgment that

I might be associating with kooks! I *knew* that I couldn't recall my own birth, and concluded that no one else could either, and simply pigeon-holed it as the idiosyncrasy of an enthusiast."

Dr. Erwin is now an avid supporter of Dr. Cheek's pioneering work in age regression. Surprisingly, the above quote is from the foreword that Dr. Erwin wrote for Dr. Cheek's book on "ideomotor signals," which are a key component of age regression—and which you'll learn more about in the pages to come.

Even Dr. David Chamberlain, a Vice President of the Prenatal and Perinatal Psychology Association of North America, and a strong supporter of Dr. Cheek's age regression work, was hesitant to share knowledge not commonly accepted by psychologists, even after he had demonstrated it in his own clinical research. Dr. Chamberlain's book, *Babies Remember Birth*, only mentions what he calls "non-ordinary states" near the end of his book. It is here that he tells his readers that "psychology slowly has been introducing us to a range of non-ordinary states where things once thought impossible are possible." He then talks about three of his own clients who displayed "feats of mind over time," his reference being to reports of reincarnation and past lives. In the appendix to his book, Dr. Chamberlain notes the following:

"My own experiences with birth memory have shown me that human consciousness is more than physical and has continuity and maturity at all ages. I find intelligent life before birth entirely real, though distinctly spiritual in nature. The most accurate description I know for life that is nonphysical but conscious is *spirit*."[2]

The purpose of this book you now hold in your hands is to share the near birth experience and what it teaches concerning the life of the spirit. The near birth experience reminds us who we are, it affirms our spiritual nature and helps us realize that our essential core is *spirit*.

The near birth experience can free you from what the culture has programmed you to think. It can help you take the *dismembered* parts of your being, the parts cut off from your soul, and *re-member* them, putting them together in ways that fit your true essence. It will present you with the memory that who you are is not primarily a human being having a spiritual experience but rather a spiritual being having a human experience.

The near birth experience has convinced me that even though the memory of who we are may be deeply buried, it is nevertheless far more accessible than previously imagined, and perhaps remarkably so. This book offers you a chance to rediscover and relive that memory. Along the way, you will be reminded that your time here on earth is intended to help you grow in love and compassion. You will discover that it is possible to remember not only your time spent in the womb before your birth, but even a time before that. You will discover what the Holy Scriptures of all major religions have told us—that life as we know it is only a portion of our total existence. You will be reminded of what the books about near death experiences have proclaimed—that you will survive this life and that there is much more to come after the death of our physical bodies.

You will find that the benefits of this book, and the near birth experience, are very much focused on the here and now. Remembering who you are liberates you to live more fully, with fewer regrets, but also with more compassion for your own and others' failures. Some of what you read may seem new and challenging to you. But if you are like most, you will also discover that these new revelations put you in touch with information you already know, wisdom that resides deep within your own soul.

This book can help you find new meaning in both your joy and your suffering, and can help you understand and fulfill your life purpose. The messages you will receive are many: You are of infinite value, and your life here on this planet is of great value. You have chosen to come here for a reason, a purpose. You are not contained or constrained by the physical boundaries of this life. What happens here, in your present life, is important, but is only part of your eternal existence, one that began before this life and will continue long after it.

In your present life, it is the path rather than the destination that is important. You can take steps every day along the path you have chosen; in fact, every decision you make will take you either further along the path or away from it. One important decision, one important step along the path, is to go to the center of your self, and this book offers a way to do this.

Much of what you will find in these pages is not particularly new. Books about the near death experience have helped many people remember their spiritual essence, and that we are all eternal beings who are connected to God. The near birth experience differs from the near death experience in that it is much easier and safer to be guided back to near birth memories than it is to experience your near death. This book will be invaluable for you as a guide in that process.

You do not need to have your own near birth experience to benefit from this book, however. The most important parts of this book come through the stories of others, whose experiences offer additional evidence for the true spiritual nature of our lives. The connection each person has with God can be illuminated by the near birth experience whether or not you directly experience your own. The message of those whose stories I offer here inspire all of us to live in accordance with who we are. Their experiences demonstrate that we can connect with the love which is and always has been at the core of our being, a love more life-giving than even the love we might feel for any single person in our lives. The way this happens is what we will explore in the rest of the book.

CHAPTER ONE

THE FULL-LENGTH MIRROR

Mulla Nasrudin goes to the bank to cash a check. The teller asks, "Do you have any identification?" The Mulla looks puzzled. "We need some identification, so we know that you are the person whose name is on the check." Nasrudin thinks for a moment, reaches into his pocket, pulls out a mirror, and peers carefully into it. "Yes, that's me!" he says.

—Sufi Parable

Working for the past nine years with the near birth experience has changed my view of what a human being is, and has expanded my view of life. It is as if I had been looking into a pocket-sized mirror, and now the mirror is as large as the room I am in, a full-length mirror reflecting a much larger life than I had ever imagined.

Like Mulla Nasrudin in the Sufi story, many of us carry a pocket-size mirror with us, in a pocket somewhere in our mind. This mirror reflects a view of life as defined by our society. It reflects who we are, but the picture we see is limited. It mirrors our body and our physical existence, but not our soul. It is the image associated with our name, our job, and our position in society. It is a way of seeing that tells us that some people are more important than others, that the life of the president is more important than the lives of the Secret Service men and women who guard him, and that somehow it is right for these bodyguards to sacrifice their lives for his if he is attacked.[1] It tells us that the lives of our enemies are of little value, that to kill them in war is a good thing. It tells us that people are valued by how much money they make, and that therefore professional athletes are more valuable than teachers or nurses. It reflects the belief that our lives are limited to the approximately eighty-six years we have from birth to death. *That's all there is*, the pocket mirror reflects to us.

THE FULL-LENGTH MIRROR

The near birth experience provides an alternative to this pocket-sized view of life, reflecting a wider vision. It is like a full-length mirror that reflects our essence, the part of self which existed even before our birth and which will exist after our death.

The near birth experience expands our view of life by presenting memories of life before birth. It helps us remember the feelings of safety and nurture we enjoyed in the warmth of our mother's body; it helps us relive the feelings of joy and freedom we had as we turned somersaults in the womb. More importantly, the near birth experience brings to our conscious awareness deeply spiritual messages about the meaning of our lives, messages from a time not only before birth, but even before our conception.

These memories remind us that every person on earth has come here with a purpose or mission to be accomplished. The near birth experience confirms Wordsworth's thought, that we come "trailing clouds of glory," sent directly from God. Memories from the near birth experience help us understand that the lack of meaning experienced by so many people in this life is due at least partly to their inability to remember who they are and why they have come here.

The near birth experience helps us remember in the deepest sense: it helps us to re-member, to put together again, the fragmented parts of our lives, the parts *dismembered* when we forgot our true identity. It helps us return to wholeness so that we might find meaning, even in our suffering.

MADELINE AND THE QUESTION OF SUFFERING

I first met Madeline at lunch. Several years before, her fiancé, George, had used the near birth experience as a part of his successful struggle to overcome his addiction to alcohol. He called to tell me that he was doing very well, and was engaged. Could I have lunch with him and the woman he was going to marry? He wanted me to perform the wedding ceremony and she needed to meet me in order to decide whether that would be okay for her.

So we had lunch, and talked about the wedding and their lives together. It was a very pleasant time, and when we left the restaurant Madeline asked if I would put the date for their wedding on my calendar.

Two days later she called me. George had suggested that she might cope better with her frequent bouts of depression if she enlisted the help of the near birth experience. He had described the process to her and told her about his own experience of regressing back not only to the womb, but also to a time before this life, a time when he was with God. He told her that experiencing God's presence of love during the near birth experience had helped him love himself enough to change, to treat himself as valuable and worthy of enjoying a healthy life. He thought the near birth experience might help her. She was skeptical, but willing to give it a try.

"I've had a lot of suffering in my life," she said after we had exchanged greetings and she was sitting in a chair at my office. "And I'm mad at God. Either he doesn't care very much about me, or else he isn't very powerful, because most of my life I've had to deal with one form of suffering or another."

Madeline told me that her older brothers had sexually abused her when she was a little girl, but her parents would not believe her when she told them. They said she must have imagined it.

She said to me, "Since I was a teenager I've had a lot of problems because of that. I haven't been to church for a long time now, and I'm not sure what I believe any more. But I would like the chance to talk to God, to let him know how mad I am at him!"

I showed her how to regress back to the womb. She cried when she relived her birth, for her mother had refused to hold Madeline when she was born, saying to the nurse, "Just take her away for now." This was upsetting to Madeline, and she spontaneously emerged from her regression and told me that her relationship with her mother had always been tumultuous, that she had always suspected her mother did not want her, and this memory of rejection at birth only confirmed for her what she already had felt for most of her life.

I suggested that she again regress to the womb, then go back as far as she could, to find her earliest or most helpful memory. She went back to a time just before labor began, and then found herself getting smaller and smaller until she was just a little speck. Soon she was in space, without a body. She took a moment to orient herself in this new situation, and then she saw the Light. I asked her to go toward it, and she did. When I asked her if she knew what this Light was, she replied "It is God."

I asked her to communicate with God, to say whatever she needed or wanted to say. She could do this either silently, or out loud so that I could hear. She was silent for a long time, perhaps four or five minutes. Then tears began streaming down her face. I waited for perhaps thirty seconds, and asked what was happening.

She told me that she had expressed her anger to God for the suffering she had endured in this life. She had said, "God, why didn't you do anything when you saw how much suffering I had as a child? How could you let such things happen?"

Then she said it was as if a veil had suddenly been lifted; she was able to view a scene of something a long time ago, as if it were happening right before her eyes, though she knew it to be a long ago memory.

* * *

She was with God, totally enveloped by the warmest light of love that could be imagined. She had said, "God, I am so overwhelmed by your love! You are so beautiful! Is there anything I can do to be more like you, to be filled with more of your love?" God had looked at her for a while, and then said, "There is a path that can allow your soul to expand to its fullest, to be able to hold more of my love and compassion. It is the path of suffering, the path taken by my son."

"I will do anything to be more like you!" she had responded, and then God had shown her the life she could choose in order to experience suffering, and to allow her to expand her soul to encompass more love.

As she sat in my office reporting this experience, she began again to weep. "Now I understand!" she said. "Now I understand!"

She said she would like to have some time to think about what she had just experienced, and asked if we could have another appointment. When we met a week later, she told me that she didn't think she was ready for marriage, that there were some things she had always wanted to do that she had never done. She wanted to travel, and then live for a while on a ranch with horses. She had talked with George about this, and they had decided to call off the wedding.

"Oh great!" I thought. I was sure George would be angry that Madeline had called off the wedding as a result of the near birth experience. And if he was angry, he would probably be angry with me. But when I called him I discovered that he wasn't angry at all. "It's for the best," he said.

He had thought marriage could help Madeline cope with her frequent bouts of depression, that his love for her would make it better, that *he* could make it better. But now he realized that he needed to let go of her for a while, to give her a chance to work out her own path. He was grateful for the way the near birth experience had helped him earlier, and how it was now helping Madeline. He said that she seemed like a new person. He could see that she seemed no longer angry or depressed, but lighter, more excited about life.

She believed now that her suffering had meaning, that suffering was a way to help her to develop love and compassion, to expand her soul. Some of the dis-membered parts of her self had been re-membered, and she felt more whole, more centered, less fragmented.

It would be wrong to think that this example implies that suffering is always good, that we should do nothing to alleviate it because it can help us. That is not the point of this example, and it is not a conclusion reached by either Madeline or me. It is true that suffering can help expand a person's soul to bring compassion and love for others who suffer, but love is even more likely to do that, and those who love seem motivated to alleviate suffering.

Our task is to bring love. That is a primary message of the near birth experience. We come from God, trailing clouds of glory. The near birth experience helps us go inside, to find that at our center we are still in touch with that memory, and with that presence.

For some, the near birth experience has offered insights or revelations that have been life-changing. How it works, how it has influ-enced the lives of people who have experienced it, and what the meaning of the near birth experience might be for you and for oth-ers who may not have experienced it directly—these are the topics of the following pages.

The message throughout these pages is this: there is meaning in life, in *every* life. What we see revealed in the pocket-sized mirror held up to us by our society is only a small part of the magnificence of our total existence.

To discover our true magnificence is a great gift, of course, but it eludes us for much of our lives. Too many of us are like Mulla Nasrudin, searching frantically for something that is not even lost:

> Mulla Nasrudin was seen galloping lickety-split through his village, as fast as his donkey could carry him. "Where are you going so quickly?" one of the villagers called out as he sped by. As he disappeared into the distance they heard his answer: "I've lost my donkey, and want to find him as fast as I can!"

The Mulla's donkey was his prized possession. It could carry him and everything he would need as he journeyed from one village to another. It could help him plow a field or carry heavy burdens to or from the market. It was a form of wealth, a form of security. To lose a donkey would be to lose something so important that it can sym-bolize for us the loss of security, the loss of wealth, the loss of peace of mind.

The near birth experience tells us that the meaning in our lives, and also the peace we seek, is within, even closer to us than Nasrudin's donkey as he galloped along on its back, frantically searching for it. Life being what it is, we sometimes need someone to tell us to slow down, to stop, to pay attention, to take a moment to recognize that what we are seeking can never be found by racing across the countryside, but by pausing to look at ourselves.

CHAPTER TWO

SEARCHING FOR THE DONKEY

Where is the I, the entity that decides what to do with the psychic energy generated by the nervous system? Where does the captain of the ship, the master of the soul, reside?

—Mihaly Csikszentmihalyi

My discovery of the near birth experience came about through what in retrospect seems a circuitous route. In 1991, I had just become the director of Chrysalis Counseling Center in Bellevue, Washington, and many of my clients suffered from symptoms of Post Traumatic Stress Disorder (PTSD).

I knew that many survivors of severe trauma are overwhelmed by the memory of that event. A veteran of the Vietnam conflict who survived attacks which killed his comrades, a woman who was raped repeatedly by her father when she was a small child, or the sole survivor of an automobile accident that killed family and friends may be flooded with guilt, fear, and other negative feelings and even thoughts of suicide.

In my search for ways to help people who had suffered such traumas, I came across an article by Dr. Leslie LeCron, a psychologist. It was titled, "A Hypnotic Technique for Uncovering Unconscious Material," published in *The International Journal of Clinical and Experimental Hypnosis* in 1954. I learned in the article that in 1929 Dr. LeCron had realized that if a person held a pendulum and let it swing while concentrating on the words "Yes, Yes, Yes," the movement of the pendulum would change when the person changed his or her thoughts to "No, No, No." By 1954 he had discovered that the combination of light hypnosis and unconscious muscular gestures could break through the amnesia that masks memories of birth, the first years of life, and the experiences of people under general anesthesia.

Dr. LeCron called the unconscious muscular gestures "ideomotor" signals, and developed finger signals that he believed were easier to work with than a pendulum. Soon after this, Dr. Milton Erickson, a psychiatrist and hypnotherapist, and Dr. David Cheek, an obstetrician and gynecologist, began using light hypnosis and ideomotor finger signals as a basis for developing a process of age regression to help expectant mothers remember or relive their own birth. Although they did not use the term "near birth experience," this is where the process began for me.

Several years after Cheek and Erickson began making their work widely available, the process of regression to the womb was found to be helpful for people who had suffered severe trauma. My interest in the treatment of severe trauma was what led me, in March of 1991, to attend a conference where Dr. Cheek was demonstrating this technique for professional counselors.

DR. DAVID CHEEK

My first impression of Dr. Cheek was of a gentle, strong man with a resonant voice. His eyes sparkled, and he betrayed a sense of humor that often brought not a belly laugh, but a soft smile to his own face and to each person in the audience. At our conference he stated that each of us has the ability to retrieve pre-birth memories with the help of ideomotor signals, and he presented evidence that memories recovered through hypnotic age regression are valid descriptions of what actually happened.[1] He had been using hypnosis since the late 1950s to help his patients deliver their babies without pain or drugs, and since 1960 he had routinely regressed his patients back to the womb to help them have empathy for and understanding of what their unborn babies were experiencing.

By the early 1980s some of the babies he had delivered were adult women who wanted him to deliver their babies. When he regressed these women back to the womb, he was then able to compare their memories with the dictated notes taken when they were born. He found that their memories matched his notes. They even remembered what doctors and other staff members said. How this could be was not clear, because a baby is not expected to understand language. And yet these women, regressed back to the moment of birth, could recall the words the doctor said, the conversations between their mother and other people in the delivery room, and what occurred in the mother's hospital room a few hours later.

Dr. Cheek told us of one woman who, when regressed to the womb and to her birth, had remembered that when her umbilical cord was cut she had grabbed Dr. Cheek's thumb, and he had said to her mother, "Your little girl has a healthy reflex!" When he checked his notes,[2] he read that the baby had grabbed his thumb, and he had told the mother that her baby's grip was strong and her reflexes were healthy. This verified the daughter's memory.

At our conference Dr. Cheek asked for volunteers to experience age regression and to demonstrate for others what it was like to remember or relive the experience of being in the womb and reliving their own births. Many who stepped forward were skeptical, but within ten to fifteen minutes they were exhibiting the body movements of a newborn baby, and reporting memories of life in the womb, the birth process, and the first moments of life.

Dr. Cheek explained that these memories have value. It is good for a person to remember being in the womb, surrounded by the rhythms of his mother's heartbeat, the warmth of her body, and the safety and nurture she provides. These memories can influence attitudes toward life, and are especially important in developing a sense of basic trust—an attitude that the world is a place of safety and nurture. When I heard this, it struck me that this could be an especially important experience for survivors of severe trauma—the very people I was seeking to help. It seemed to me that the early memory of being loved and welcomed into the world might provide enough security to help such people confront their fears enough to recover from trauma.

At the conference Dr. Cheek told of how excited people were about recovering memories of life in the womb and the first hours of life. They were amazed to discover that, "I was the one who started labor, by pushing with my feet against the womb, because I was too big and too cramped to stay there." Or they remember being brought to their mother after the delivery: "Dad was there, and he looked so young and so proud. He had a suit on, and a tie, and he hardly ever wore a suit and tie. And he had a crew cut, and he was smiling."

I was so impressed by Dr. Cheek's demonstration that I began to use this technique with my clients. I wanted to provide these people with their early memories of being safe and loved while in the womb. I hoped that these memories would have enough power to produce and maintain a sense of safety and security, enough to substantially diminish the negative thoughts and feelings triggered by the trauma. Perhaps the early memories of being in the womb would help relieve the symptoms of Post-Traumatic Stress Disorder.

In fact the process did help. But I soon learned that the near birth experience had an additional value, one that could benefit nearly everyone in ways I could not have guessed. As I gained experience with this procedure, I was amazed to discover something Dr. Cheek had not demonstrated at our conference.[3] I learned that some people spontaneously remembered not only being in the womb, but also a time even before that—a time before this life, a time when they are[4] with a bright light, which they refer to as God.

They were invariably surprised to discover that they do not have a body during this time before entering the womb. They may experience the presence of other out-of-body people whom they recognize as friends, either from this life or a previous one. They may remember speaking with these friends about the journey they were about to take into this world. Their memory of being with God remained with them even as babies in the womb. They reported that while in the womb they are conscious, aware not only of the memory of being with God, but aware of their mother's state of mind. They could hear and understand much of what she says, and could understand conversations she had with other people.

At birth the situation changes. Most people forget about God and pretty much lose their ability to understand conversations. Some people forget within hours after birth, but apparently some people retain the memory of being with God until about the time they are able to begin reading, at which time they forget all of their pre-birth experiences.

It is important to know that the forgetting is only on a conscious level, as seems to be true of all forgetting. Everything that happens to us, whether before or after birth, remains stored in the unconscious mind, or somewhere, and much of this material can be brought into conscious awareness by the near birth experience.[5]

What was surprising to discover was that the memories of being with God before this life tend to be even more powerful than the memories of safety in the womb. The memory of a time with God before conception provides a deep sense of safety along with a clear understanding of the meaning and purpose of life. For those who experienced trauma in the womb, the near birth experience provides memories of their earliest experiences of love, of a time before being in the womb and therefore of a time before trauma.

Many people who have experienced near birth view life differently thereafter. They understand their time on earth as a journey of the soul which began before this life and which will continue after the death of their present body. As a result of the near birth experience many people no longer view the earth as their only home, but view this life from birth to death as only part of their journey, their time on earth only a station along the way. The values of our society no longer appear as absolute to them, or even in any way compelling. Money and material goods no longer seem as important as the life of the Spirit.

Moreover, people who have had a near birth experience come away from it with a very different perspective of every person they know. They view all of life in a different light. The near birth experience helps a person remember that each and every person is a soul in the image and likeness of God—a mirror reflecting the presence of God. Following a near birth experience, the old person in a nursing home, the homeless person on the street, and the billionaire are all viewed as of equal value, of the same "stuff," all on the same path, coming from God and returning to God again after this life.

As I immersed myself in this work, I realized that the messages of all the near birth experiences I'd witnessed resonated deeply within my own soul. They were somehow more real and more important than any of the messages that contradicted them. The near birth experience conveyed the same message as the words written by Marianne Williamson and spoken by Nelson Mandela in his 1994 inaugural address:

> You are a child of God. Your playing small doesn't serve the world. There is nothing enlightened about shrinking so that other people won't feel insecure around you. We were born to manifest the glory of God that is within us. It's not just in some of us, it is in everyone. And as we let our own light shine, we unconsciously give other people permission to do the same. As we are liberated from our fear, our presence automatically liberates others. . . .[6]

The universal message of the near birth experience is that God is directly available to each of us, and every single one of us is created as a channel of God's love and grace. We all are born to manifest the glory of God within us.

The memories from the near birth experience indicate that our time in the womb, for most people, is very much like being in Eden, where God is present, where we are safe, nourished, warm, and surrounded by love. The near birth experience also suggests that when we are in the womb we are very much like Adam and Eve. We are fully conscious in the same way adults are fully conscious, not a blank slate as many think of a baby or fetus. We carry with us the memory of God and of our purpose in life. To paraphrase a popular book title, *All I Ever Needed to Know I Learned In Kindergarten*, the near birth experience suggests that "All I Really Needed to Know I Learned Before I Was Born."[7]

The near birth experience helps us remember.

CHAPTER THREE

MEMORIES FROM THE WOMB?

Before I formed you in the womb I knew you,
Before you were born I set you apart;
I appointed you as a prophet to the nations.

—Jeremiah 1:5

M y first indication of just how important the near birth experience could be in helping us connect with the life of the spirit was in May of 1991, just two months after I had attended Dr. Cheek's seminar. A therapist who helps her clients deal with abuse came to see me in order to learn how to regress her clients to the womb. She had heard about this process and wanted to experience it for herself, in order to evaluate its appropriateness for her counseling practice. So, using the procedure I learned from Dr. Cheek, I helped her regress to a time before her birth. She described being in the womb, and described it as warm, safe, and comfortable.

For some reason that I still don't understand, I deviated slightly from the procedure I had learned, and instead of proceeding to the beginning of labor and then to the birth, I asked her if she had an earlier memory. I expected that she might move to a time a few weeks earlier in the pregnancy. However, what she said was, "There is nothing there."

At first I thought she literally meant that her mind was a blank, that there were no earlier memories, that there was nothing there. But then I remembered my training and instead of assuming I knew what she meant, I asked her, "What do you mean, nothing is there?" That's when I found out that she was experiencing being in empty space. Her mother's body was no longer there. She was experiencing infinite space and remembering an out-of-body experience.

Her eyes were closed. I asked her to keep them closed, but to look around. Somehow she knew what I meant and she visually explored that empty space. Then she saw the Light. She noticed it far in the distance, a Bright Light. I asked her to go toward it, and she did (mentally); that's when she discovered it was God. As she approached the Light she became overwhelmed with a sense of unconditional love, and tears began to flow down her face. She talked of the experience of total freedom she felt while in the presence of the Light, a freedom she still had when I talked with her a week later. She felt freer to be her true self, and she understood that this self was good, was in some sense *perfect*.

Since then I have suggested the near birth experience as a way— first for my clients and later for my friends—to get in touch with inner resources of which they might not yet be aware. For those who take me up on the offer I now routinely ask each of them, when they are regressed to the womb, "Do you have an earlier memory?" Following are some examples of the way the near birth experience has been a help.

FRENCH FRIES AND MEMORIES OF CRISIS

Ray, Pam, and their fifteen-year-old son were having a meal at McDonald's restaurant after a day of skiing in the Cascade Mountains in Washington. It had been a great day. The snow was perfect, and they enjoyed being together outdoors. While they ate Big Macs and French fries, their conversation was sprinkled with laughter and good-natured banter. Then suddenly Pam started to cry, and Ray knew why, though their son was puzzled.

The French fry machine was emitting a "beep beep beep" sound to indicate that the fries were ready. But both Ray and Pam flashed back to a time seventeen years earlier, at a neonatal intensive care unit. Their baby, Christie, was hooked up to wires and tubes where she lay critically ill. Suddenly they heard a beeping sound in the room. The nurses ran in and asked them to leave the room. The doctors came running and then Christie died. The French fry machine was making the same, godawful beeping noise they had heard that day. When it didn't stop, Ray got up and screamed at the girl behind the counter, *"Shut off that machine!"*

A few days later Ray was in my office asking for help to deal with emotions he had stuffed down for almost seventeen years, but which wouldn't stay buried anymore. We used a process called Traumatic Incident Reduction (TIR),[1] which helped him uncover and discharge the emotions related to the trauma. Before he left my office that day, I told him about the near birth experience. He decided to try it during our next session the following week. Using ideomotor signals, he regressed back to the womb, and then to a time just before he entered his body.

He recognized other people there, bidding him farewell, and he found himself on a journey that passed by a playground. There were children in the playground. One of them was Christie. She was bathed in a white light, and somehow he knew that she was still alive—that she was alive before this life, and was alive after it! This experience relieved his pain, because now he felt more connected to her. She was no longer dead, but alive in spirit. Maybe he would see her again. For her, death was not the end of existence, but a transition from the physical body to something else; something freer.

The near birth experience gave Ray a new way of viewing the world. It does that for many people, not just for those who have suffered trauma. I learned something important from Ray. I had often questioned, and still do, the role of suffering in our lives. From Ray I learned that sometimes suffering can expand our soul, as God had suggested to Madeline (see Chapter One).

One day when Ray was taking a walk in his neighborhood, he noticed a FOR SALE sign in his neighbor's yard. He knocked on the door. When the neighbor answered Ray introduced himself, saying that he lived nearby. Having noticed the FOR SALE sign, he wondered what was happening. The neighbor replied, "We've had our little boy in the hospital for the past six months, and our insurance won't cover it all. So we have to sell our house to pay the bills. We don't know yet where we'll go."

When Ray went home, he told his wife about this conversation, and they decided they would take money out of their savings account and give it to the neighbor to help the family stay in their house. I didn't find out precisely how much money they gave, but it was enough to allow the neighbor to stay in their home. Of course I don't know for sure, but I think that if Ray and Pam had not suffered the loss of their own child, they may not have had as much compassion. I know that not every neighbor who knew of the situation responded so generously.

BILL — ONE IN A HUNDRED

Bill[2] is a professional person and has become a close friend of mine. He and his wife have two children, and life is going very well for them. He had heard reports from other people of their near birth experience and he wanted to go back to his own birth experience. During his first session Bill easily learned the use of ideomotor signals and regressed to the womb rather quickly. He focused on the experience of being welcomed by his mother during his birth. This involved considerable emotion for him, because his mother had died when Bill was nine years old. At my suggestion he then reentered the womb. It was my hope that he would be able to remember the time before his birth. When asked to go back to his earliest memory in this life, he was silent for a long time, his eyes closed. When he opened his eyes he reported the following:

"I don't know if I remember this or if I imagined it, but I could see myself sitting on God's lap and realizing that it was time to be born. I felt a little bit afraid. I told God it looks scary down there and I don't know if I'm ready. But God didn't answer. Instead, He started to play with a top. The spinning top looked a lot like the planet Earth, from a long distance away."

Bill talked about what this experience meant to him. He viewed the top as a metaphor. In order to stay balanced the top has to be centered. He thought God was telling him to stay balanced and centered. He also felt that God was showing him that the Earth gets its energy from God.

He paused for a while, and then asked if he could go back to this early time again, sitting on the lap of God. I asked him to close his eyes and go back there, and to let me know what he experienced. Once again he was silent for a while, and I waited. A few minutes later he reported what had happened:

"I was sitting in God's lap, and I could feel God's joy for me and I responded with my own joy. Then God reached to his left and handed me a large stick with a banner attached. On the banner was written one word: *Hope*."

When he saw the banner, Bill knew intuitively that this was his calling, to bring hope to a world where so many people seemed to be living lives of quiet desperation. He thought he could do this best by being like the top, to "live life out of my center, to remain balanced, and to stay in relationship with God, my source of energy." He thought for a minute, and then added, "Spinning a top is also a way to play. I think God wants me to find a lot more time in life to play, to have more fun instead of taking it all too seriously."

I know Bill quite well. He already is a banner of hope for many people. Sometimes he does find it difficult to take time to play, and it is important for him to live a centered and balanced life. He takes seriously, and playfully, the messages of the near birth experience. He regularly takes time to connect with God through meditation and prayer, and he often communicates with God.

On one occasion he felt God say to him, "Bill, you are one in a hundred." Bill was confused. "Don't you mean one in a *million*?" he asked. But the answer was no, he was one in a hundred. When Bill thought that over, he began to get some ideas about it. He thought about what it would be like if in churches or other organizations every hundred people became a group and adopted someone who needed help. Maybe they could adopt a single parent with young children. Maybe someone in a nursing home. Maybe a homeless person. If each of the hundred people gave one dollar per day or one dollar per one hundred dollars of income; or if they gave one hour out of every hundred hours to help someone else, even one hour a week, it could change many lives. He thought about being one in a hundred, and began talking to pastors about a program like that.

Bill has become the head of a non-profit organization in the city of

Seattle, one that is combining resources of churches, business, and city government to help inspire people with a vision. He has received a grant of more than a million dollars from the Kellogg Foundation and the support of many individuals and organizations in the Seattle area, and he and his organization are making a positive impact on the city, so much so that the city of Seattle declared December 3, 1998 as "Center for Ethical Leadership Day" in honor of the impact Bill and his center have had.

To be with Bill or others during the near birth experience is amazing, energizing, and inspiring, not only for them, but also for me. When a person encounters God during the near birth experience, the emotional atmosphere in the room shifts dramatically—the presence of the Light frequently brings tears. This encounter with the Light usually begins as a pre-birth memory, but soon it changes and the memory becomes a here-and-now event. The person experiencing the near birth experience can now talk with God, ask questions, and receive answers.

It is difficult to describe the release people find in their tears of joy, or sometimes tears of sorrow or regret as they experience the near birth experience. For one man the Bright Light, like a fireball, became the face of Jesus, who was wearing a crown of thorns. Seeing this vision, he began to cry silently, tears flowing down his cheeks. He had recently been diagnosed with a very serious illness, and he understood the crown of thorns to be a symbol for what he would experience during the illness. At the same time he knew that God was with him in the room, and would be with him during his illness, and this gave him strength.

For him the message of the near birth experience is that the soul is our essence, and that our essence is good. For him and for many others, the words of Wordsworth's poem became a statement of reality: that we come from God "trailing clouds of glory" and we will return to God, a being of Love and Light. Though we leave our body, we never die.

CHAPTER FOUR

IDEOMOTOR FINGER SIGNALS
AND THE INNER VOICE

A neighbor came to ask Mulla Nasrudin if he could borrow his donkey. "I'm sorry, I have already lent my donkey to someone else," the Mulla replied. But just then a donkey brayed. The sound came from Nasrudin's stable. "But Mulla, I just heard your donkey bray, and the sound came from in there!" As the Mulla shut the door on his neighbor, he said indignantly, yet with great dignity, "Anyone who would take the word of a donkey over the word of a Mulla certainly is not worth being able to borrow my donkey!"

L ike Mulla Nasrudin's neighbor, we are often confronted with conflicting information, and often the conflict is between an inner and an outer voice. It is the dilemma of a Sufi saying, attributed to Haidar Asari:

> *A voice whispered to me last night:*
> *"There is no such thing as a voice whispering in the night."*[1]

What are we to do? Which evidence is convincing enough for us to let it influence our view of reality or a decision to act? Do we listen to the donkey or to the Mulla, to the voice whispering in the night or to the message it contains telling us to discount the voice, that indeed there is no such thing as a voice whispering in the night?

The advice of the near birth experience is very clear on this issue. We are to listen to the inner voice, to the braying of Nasrudin's donkey rather than the voice of the Mulla; the inner voice rather than the external voice of authority. To listen to the Mulla rather than the voice of the donkey could lead us astray.

These messages from the stable, which are symbolic of the messages from our unconscious mind, can be more important or ultimately more convincing than the external voices which might contradict them, even if the external voices come from a Mulla or other authority. Yet too often when we hear the still quiet voice within, we ignore it—drowning it out with the louder external voices of authority or tradition, which flood our consciousness.

Ideomotor signals help us pay more attention to the wisdom that comes from within. Though we might not know them by this name, ideomotor signals are familiar to us all.

When I was in grade school I used to go to a Saturday matinee at the local movie theater. One hero I remember was a soft-spoken cowboy movie star who drank sarsaparilla instead of whiskey. Whenever he got mad, whenever he was about to swing into action against the bad guys, he would take a stick of gum out of his pocket and start chewing. That was a sign that things were going to get exciting. Usually the bad guys did not recognize the signal, but all of us kids in the theater did, and the noise level in the increasingly excited crowd intensified every time.

We're all a little like this cowboy in that we each have our own way of signaling what is going on in our thoughts or feelings. A good salesman begins to recognize how we do that, whether we are aware of what we are doing or not. Our head might nod when we are in agreement with someone. Our breathing might change, our heartbeat might quicken, or we might run our hands through our hair.

When we use an unconscious muscular movement to signal something about our thoughts or feelings, this is called an "ideomotor signal." Sometimes these signals are so subtle, with the most minuscule movements, that they easily pass from our attention without recognition. That is why ideomotor finger signals are important. They bring unconscious information to our conscious awareness.

Ideomotor signals are crucial resources for the near birth experience since they can tell us when things are going on in our unconscious mind, things that we might otherwise deny or not recognize.

Birth memories and encounters with the divine are indeed subtle at times, often buried beneath memories and concerns of a seemingly more urgent nature. For this reason ideomotor signals are the perfect tool for leading us back to these memories, bringing them to light so that we can make use of them in our everyday lives. In Sara's story, the value of these subtle messages charted our way deep into the psyche, where she had buried secrets from herself.

SARA AND THE INNER WISDOM

When Sara was four years old she found a box of wooden matches beside the living-room fireplace. Though she had been forbidden to play with matches, she lit one. She remembers this event clearly, because her father caught her at it and decided to teach her a lesson. He took the box of matches, lit one, and held her right hand over the flame until her flesh blistered. "That will teach you not to play with matches!" he had said.

Now Sara is thirty years old. For most of her life she had thought of herself as stupid and bad, always doing something she would get punished for. There were so many rules, and it seemed she was always breaking one. It seemed she couldn't do anything right. It had never occurred to her that some of the rules of her childhood might have been too strict, too arbitrary, or the punishments too severe. But lately she had begun to acknowledge her anger toward her father, including a fantasy about shooting him. She was also angry with her mother for never protecting her, never stepping between her and her stern, uncompromising father. Sara decided to come for counseling to learn how to deal with her anger.

Sara's first question was about her father. She wanted to know if I thought he was abusive. I told her that her perceptions about her father were more important than mine. On some level she already knew the answer to her question. I asked her what she thought. "I don't know," she said. "He was pretty strict, but I don't know if he was abusive. He probably did it for my own good."

Since she seemed in conflict about this answer I suggested she might learn how to get answers from a deeper level. I taught her ideomotor finger signals.

She was sitting down. I asked her to put her hands on her knees where she could watch them, and to think "Yes," to fill her head with "*Yes!*" Then I told her to ask her hands to select a "yes" finger. She would know which finger because it would become lighter than the rest, or heavier, or it would feel cold or hot, or tingle, or somehow attract her attention. The finger which would *seem to be* the "yes" finger would in fact be the "yes" finger, and she could move it or let it move itself. Sara's "yes" finger turned out to be the forefinger of her right hand.

Next I asked her to find a "no" finger, and then a finger to signal "I don't know" or "I don't want to tell you." I told her to ask the fingers if they would be willing to help her discover some information from within herself. Within thirty seconds the "yes" finger moved. We had now set up exactly what we needed for getting accurate ideomotor signals.

Next it was time to use these signals to help her find an answer to her question about whether her father was abusive. So I told Sara to ask herself, "Do I believe that my father was abusive to me?"

She asked the question. None of her fingers moved. After about a minute I asked her what was happening. The answer she gave was startling:

She said, "The finger on my right hand wanted to move, to say, 'Yes.' But I suddenly could see, in my imagination, my left hand grabbing a knife and stabbing my right hand and pinning it to the chair so it couldn't move, and a voice inside my head shouted at me saying, 'You can't talk against your Dad!' "

Part of Sara knew that her dad was abusive, and she wanted to be able to talk about that. The "yes" finger wanted to move, but another part of her fought to keep her from revealing the truth. To speak would be to betray her family, and she had been trained never to do that.

However, inside she knew. The fingers tried to signal yes, her father was abusive, that what he did was harmful rather than helpful and good. But coercion and fear made it difficult for her to get in touch with what she knew.

I told her I had a question I would like to ask of her innermost self, and I wanted her fingers to answer for us. I asked, "Is Sara bad or stupid, in her essence?"

Immediately her "no" finger answered. On one level she had taken in the labels put there by her father, but on a deeper level she knew differently.

We often lead our lives influenced by the negative messages given to us by people like Sara's father (or by other authority figures) rather than listening to our own deeper wisdom. It may be a teacher telling us that we are stupid, a church telling us that everyone who does not believe what we believe is headed for Hell, or a government that tells us that it is okay to drop bombs on civilians as a way to win a war.

But we don't have to let other people do our thinking for us; we don't have be wedded forever to our abusers, regardless who they are. There is a deeper wisdom of our soul that springs from a time when we had a clearer vision of ourselves. And it is possible to retrieve that memory, to recover our own truth.

Ideomotor signals help us get in touch with this inner truth. They allow a person to be in touch with the wisdom of the inner self. They are a way to focus attention, a way to listen to the inner voice. In this way they are like prayer or meditation. They are similar to the technique John Bradshaw uses when he encourages people to write to the inner child and then write the response from that inner place.[2] They help a person be in touch with the same messages that Neale Donald Walsch writes about as he sits with a pencil and paper and has a dialogue with God.[3]

Ideomotor finger signals establish a two-way communication system between the conscious and the unconscious parts of your being, allowing your mind to communicate with your soul. For some people this is rather easy; for others it is more difficult. If you are a person who believes that truth comes from an authority figure such as a Mulla, the president, the Pope, or from the Church, then it is likely that whenever your own inner self has disagreed with the president, the Pope, or the Church, then you have probably put down the inner voice and listened to the outer one. You will discount the braying of the donkey you want to borrow.

If you have been in the habit of doing this, then the inner voice has likely become so quiet that you will have trouble hearing it now. But it is still there, and ideomotor finger signals can help you connect with that inner self.

Sometimes a person may be content to establish ideomotor signals and to use them for purposes other than the near birth experience. That was the case with Sara, and is for many people. They may want to use them to help them with decision-making. Is it best for me to stay with the job I have? Is it better for me to find a different job? Or, is it better to retire?

Notice that when a person uses ideomotor finger signals for decision making, the question must always be put to the unconscious mind in such a way that when one of the fingers moves you will understand the answer. The question must therefore always be phrased so that a "yes," a "no," or an "I don't know" can be meaningful. For instance, if I ask, "Should I stay with my present job, or should I retire?" it would not particularly be helpful for the "yes" finger to move. It would be better to ask just part of the question: "Should I retire?"

For ideomotor signals to be of value there must be an honest attempt to listen to the advice of the inner self. If I want to do something that is against my best interests, for instance have an affair or buy something I clearly cannot afford, then it is important not to override the finger signals, which can advise against the desired action. Only if you trust this process will it be of value for you. It is not like flipping a coin where you can say, "I didn't like this answer, let's try for two out of three!"

* * *

For the near birth experience, establishing specific ideomotor finger signals is important and necessary, but it is only the first step. Once the finger signals have been established, it is important to test the willingness of the inner self to communicate with the conscious mind. I have found that the best way to do this is just to ask: "Are you willing to help and to guide [name of person] by providing answers to the questions we might have? Please answer by moving the appropriate finger."

At this point we watch for a finger movement, usually a twitching of a finger. If the "yes" finger moves, we know that we can proceed. If the "no" finger moves, we quit the procedure with a "thank you" to the inner self.

Above all, it is important to follow the guidance of the ideomotor finger signals, so if they give an indication that this is not the right time, or that this procedure is one they are not willing to participate in, then it is important to stop. The welfare of the person must be the primary consideration, and it is my experience that the inner self is to be trusted about what is safe and what is of benefit.

If, and only if, the "yes" finger has signaled a willingness to be of service, then it is possible to move on with the process of regressing to the womb.

CHAPTER FIVE

REGRESSION TO THE WOMB

I break up through the skin of awareness a thousand times a day, as dolphins burst through seas, and dive again, and rise, and dive.

—Annie Dillard

W e begin the journey back to the womb by asking the inner self if it is safe to proceed. This is done with the simple and direct question, "Is it safe and helpful for us now to begin the process of age regression back to the womb? Will you help us with this process?" If the "no" finger responds, we do not attempt the process, though we might ask, "Would you be willing to help us do this at a later time?" Then allow yourself to be guided by the answer to that question. We proceed with moving back in time only if the "yes" finger indicates a willingness to help, and an indication that the procedure is safe.

The reason for being so careful about this phase of the work is that some people have had traumatic experiences either while in the womb or during the birth process. This is common enough that Otto Rank has named "birth trauma" as an experience of many people. For some people, it is best not to have to deal with what is there, at least not yet, not without a trusted therapist who can help them through the traumatic memories.

Let me elaborate on this point, for it is an important one. I have known therapists who have believed that it is *always* important to confront issues, whether or not the client agrees that she is ready. But it is my experience that the best therapists develop a respectful caution about when to push, and they recognize that each of us moves toward self-knowledge at our own pace. Pushing through "resistance" in order to gain knowledge is not always wise. The near birth experience is based on the idea that it is always better to be guided by the subtle wisdom of the inner self, and that ideomotor signals must always be heeded.

> *To find knowledge, go within.*
> *To find knowledge by going without*
> *Is to go without the knowledge.*

THE BUFFALO AND THE COW

Long ago the plains of the prairies in what is now the United

States were so covered with buffalo that it could take days for a herd of them to pass by a particular spot. There were millions of them. They were great shaggy beasts. Whenever dark storm clouds gathered, whenever lightning flashed and thunder crashed and the winds became like a blizzard, the buffalo would turn their massive heads into the storm, and would weather it out by slowly walking into the midst of it, always heading into the storm. This tended to make their coats even more massive, providing even more protection as the generations went by. Those with heavy coats survived better than the others and produced more baby buffalo, so in time all the buffalo were truly magnificent beasts.

But in time the white settlers came. They not only killed the buffalo, but also brought cows with them. It was the practice of the cows to turn tail when the storm hit, to run to the safety of the barn. Some people think the word "coward" comes from the behavior of the cow.[1]

This story seems to suggest that we should all be buffalo and face into whatever storms might threaten us, that otherwise we will be cowards. And unfortunately, many therapists are of this opinion. They want to push their clients into facing whatever might be there, regardless how traumatic. But that is not how the near birth experience works. We are not all like buffalo. Some of us—perhaps most of us—are more like the cows. We may need shelter when the storms come in. We do not all have the same protections, like the buffalo with their shaggy coats.

The near birth experience respects our individual ways of responding. After all, there are now more cows than buffalo on the face of the earth. The survival mechanism of the cow has worked as well for them as its massive coat has worked for the buffalo. We are not all the same.

There is no better guide for what we should do than the inner self. That is why we ask and trust the wisdom of the ideomotor signals. To push a person to confront something when the ideomotor signals say not to is both foolhardy and disrespectful of this deeper source of knowledge. Those who do not trust the ideomotor signals are violating a basic rule of the near birth experience, and are asking for trouble.

In my experience it is helpful to have a counselor or other trusted person guide you through this process if you want to take this second step of the near birth experience. In that case the counselor or helping person asks, "Is it all right for [name] to remember the earliest events of life in the womb, and even before?" Note that the question is phrased in a very particular way. Ordinarily we would ask, "[Name], is it all right for you to remember the earliest events of life in the womb, and even before?" But in the near birth experience we address the question directly to your unconscious mind: "Is it all right for [name] to remember the earliest events of life in the womb, and even before?"

It is usually safe and can ordinarily provide helpful information if you decide to do this process without the help of another person. But remember: if—*and only if*—the ideomotor signals give you a definite "yes." Then, and only then, can you proceed with the second step.

Be patient with the process, understanding that if you don't get a clear "yes" today, you might get one tomorrow or next week or next month. I remember working with one man, Frank, who had been referred to me by another client. He had never done any kind of therapy or growth work and was quite nervous about it.

He said he would like to have me guide him through the near birth experience. But when we asked, the ideomotor signals indicated that it either was not safe or that the unconscious mind was not willing to help with the regression to the womb. Frank was disappointed but agreed to trust what his unconscious mind was telling us.

We talked about what was going on in his life. What came up was a very emotional outpouring for him. He had fought in Vietnam and had experienced events that he had never shared with anyone else in his life, as well as events only those close to him knew about. As a new second lieutenant, he had been responsible for a group of men watching a perimeter that had been overrun by Viet Cong. He saw a flash of light and then woke up in a body bag, hearing someone say, "Wait, I think this one is still alive." He seemed more ready to confront his Vietnam memories than to proceed with the near birth experience, so I suggested we try another procedure, called Traumatic Incident Reduction (TIR).[2]

He agreed, and after several sessions we decided to ask again about the near birth experience. This time the ideomotor signals said yes, and the session was very productive.

Ultimately, the benefits derived from the near birth experience depend on a basic trust in the relationship between the person being guided and the person guiding. (If you are guiding the process for yourself, this means loving, trusting, and caring for yourself. You must know that the person doing the guiding—yourself or someone else—has your best interests at heart.) To gain that trust, the guide needs to be fully committed to your welfare. Curiosity about what might happen in a regression to a previous lifetime or to a time with God before this life must never take precedence over the guidance of the ideomotor signals. If the no finger indicates you should stop, then you must stop.

When the "yes" finger indicates that the inner self will help with this process of regression to the womb, and that this process is safe, then I ask the person to close his or her eyes and imagine what it would be like to be in the womb. "What would it feel like to be in the womb? What about the temperature? What position would you likely be in? What might you hear? What would the experience be like?" I ask them to talk about anything that comes to mind regarding this experience, and they usually say something like, "Well, it would probably be dark, and warm. Maybe I could hear my mother's heartbeat." Sometimes they talk about being upside down, or turning somersaults.

I ask them to talk about anything they might experience, and to let the "yes" finger respond when what comes to mind is a memory rather than imagination. For most people who have gone this far in the process, the unconscious mind accepts this suggestion and interprets it in a meaningful way. After a while the "yes" finger will move as they talk about some experience, such as remembering the womb as a moist environment, or when they hear sounds of the amniotic fluids surrounding them, or of mother's heartbeat.

When the "yes" finger moves, I usually ask them to go to the point when labor begins, and to note who begins that process. Most of the time they report that they initiate the labor process by kicking against the womb or stretching.

Then I ask if it is safe and okay to move through the birth process. If the ideomotor signals agree that it is safe to do this, we move through the process of birth and the first moments of life outside the womb, asking the person to report what is happening each step of the way. Sometimes there is considerable energy involved at a particular moment, such as the time when the baby is first handed to mother in the delivery room. But each person responds differently.

Many people are surprised that their near birth experience has been so vivid, and that they have had such strong emotions connected with this experience. "It was so real, but I must have imagined some of it. How could I have understood what my mother said when I was born?"

The experience of well-being, of joy and of freedom while in the womb is common. And some are shocked by their memories. I particularly recall the comments of one woman, Dolores, who during the near birth experience reported that "there is another person here." I quickly learned that she was not talking about her mother.

Rather, she said that she distinctly felt the presence of another person in the womb with her, and that this person said goodbye to her shortly before they were born. The memory was so vivid that Dolores felt that she had to follow through and try to find an explanation for this. She had a meeting with her mother and Dolores told her about what she had experienced. It was only then that her mother shared with her what had happened: Dolores had had a twin! However, the twin had been stillborn. As far as mother or daughter could recall, Dolores's mother had never told her about this twin and its fate.

THE FOUNDATION FOR FURTHER WORK

As you no doubt are beginning to see, regressing to the womb is an important step of the near birth experience because it brings to mind the earliest memories of this life, memories that are usually safe and nurturing. The ability to remember these early memories prepares the way for memories of other experiences, even earlier than your present life. Beyond the experience of the womb, the near birth experience can take us into the memory of a time before the soul entered our physical bodies. This is usually the most impactful part of the near birth experience for most people. It is here that we may encounter the Bright Light, which we experience as God. It is here that we may meet directly with God and encounter a love that we have never before enjoyed so thoroughly in our lives.

CHAPTER SIX

RETURN TO THE INTERLIFE

Spirituality is the sacred center out of which all life comes, including Mondays and Tuesdays and rainy Saturday afternoons in all their mundane and glorious detail. . . . The spiritual journey is the soul's life commingling with ordinary life.

—Christina Baldwin

I magine being free, out-of-body, existing as pure spirit in perfect communication with a Being of Light. Even the one-time memory of such an experience could transform your life here on Earth. You may remember Bill, who found himself on the lap of God, contemplating the distant Earth spinning like a top in the vast, endless space. People who have gone through such experiences feel loved, perhaps as never before, and this makes a huge difference in the way they relate to the world. Their self-esteem grows noticeably. They are likely to find meaning in whatever pain or suffering they have had, and they are better able to tackle difficult situations. They lose their fear of life and their fear of death, finding meaning and a zest for living each day. Stories of such people inspire us and also provide clear evidence of how the revelations of these near birth experiences can change the way we experience our everyday lives.

PHYLLIS FINDS NEW HOPE

Phyllis was part of a group of adolescents who met with me weekly during the school year at her high school. I had been asked to facilitate this group so it could be a resource for students who had been in trouble either with the law, with the school authorities, or with their family or neighborhood. Phyllis fit all of these categories. I liked Phyllis. She always had an opinion about everything and never hesitated sharing it.

During one group session Phyllis said she didn't care what happened to her. If she got AIDS, so what? Life wasn't that great anyway. She lived with her mother. Her father was presently out of the country, but had called to tell her he would be back in time to celebrate her sixteenth birthday—a birthday that had already taken place two days earlier. He had forgotten the correct date. This had hurt Phyllis and made her angry, because it was yet more evidence to show her how little he cared. She had seen him only three times since the divorce four years earlier.

Phyllis was sexually attracted to men about ten years older than her. She stated that she hated kids, and if she ever got pregnant she would immediately have an abortion. I asked her if she thought she had a purpose in life, and she acted as if this were a ridiculous question. "Life has no meaning," she said.

I told her that I disagreed with her, that there were likely some things she had forgotten, and if she were willing to remember, I would help her. It would require taking her back to a time before she was born. "Do it!" she said, with a look that clearly challenged that possibility.

So I asked the others to be quiet or to leave the room so that Phyllis would not be distracted. Most of them were curious, and stayed. They even stayed quiet, which for that group was an unusual accomplishment.

I first took a moment to teach her ideomotor signals, and then regressed her back to the womb. She talked about it being dark and warm, and she could see something that seemed red. Her "yes" finger began to move. I asked her what position she was in, and she said her head was down. She was sucking her thumb, and it tasted salty. Soon she began describing the pressure and movement as she journeyed through the birth canal, and then her head came out.

She described the events just after birth. She talked of being laid against her mother's breast, and drinking the warm milk. She paused, and then said, "That's it!" She had spontaneously emerged from the age regression. She thought we were finished at that point. But we still had step three. We had only finished steps one and two of the near birth experience.

I asked her to go back into the womb, back to a time when she knew something she has since forgotten, something to do with her purpose in life. She was curious about this, and soon was back in the womb. I asked her to go back still further. Suddenly she seemed surprised, and I asked her what was happening. "I'm on a fluffy cloud," she said. "It's like when I took LSD." She described looking down on the earth and seeing her father in a bar, and being attracted to him. But she somehow knew that her attraction to him was not so that he could help her, but that she could help him.

She paused for a while, and then said, "I'm supposed to have a family!" She was with the Being of Light. He was helping her understand that if she found someone very different from her own father who would be willing to love and nurture children, that she could be very happy as a mother. Her task would be to love. She seemed dazed, and didn't want to talk about her experience in front of her classmates. She asked if she could see me at my office.

We met two days later. She wanted to know if she had the I.Q. to allow her to succeed at college. I administered an I.Q. "test" (The Wechsler Adult Intelligence Scale) which showed she had above average intelligence. She had decided that she wanted to go to college, and now that she knew her intelligence was high enough to do the work at college, she was going to apply.

She didn't talk with me any more about the near birth experience, but it clearly had influenced her, and it also had strengthened her relationship with me. She invited me to her high school graduation, and came to see me at my office several times during the summer and during her first year of college. We would have a cup of cocoa and talk. Her life still has many difficulties, but now she is a college student and is getting slightly better than average grades. Her relationship with her father is still problematic, but she has hope for a life with love and meaning. There are probably many reasons why her life now includes this hope. The near birth experience is one.

BREAKING THE CYCLE OF ABUSE

We have all the obstacles we need in order to reach our goals

This quote, which I saw on a bumper sticker, is a good introduction to Andrew. He came to see me about a year after his divorce. He was depressed, and didn't think there was much meaning in his life. He had quit his job and was supporting himself with the money from the sale of his house.

He was having flashbacks from when he was about eight or nine years old. He remembered his father coming into his bedroom, a room he shared with his older sister, age ten or eleven, and with his younger brother, age six or seven. Andrew slept on the bottom bunk and his sister on the top bunk of a bed. His brother slept in a separate bed.

Andrew remembered his father coming many times into the room in the middle of the night. Andy would pretend to be asleep. The door would creak, then there would be sounds of footsteps coming across the room, and then there would be a shape and sounds of the father climbing the ladder of the bunk bed. Andrew would hear the bed creak, would watch in the darkness as the top bunk sagged toward him, and he would hear his sister say, "No Dad, please don't do this."

She would say it softly, and she would whimper as Dad would say, "Well, you have your choice. I have poison here that you can take instead." And then the bed would begin to creak, and Andy would want to take his feet and kick up and knock his dad out of the bed so that his head would crack open, but he was afraid. Afraid that his dad would kill him and everyone else in the family. Afraid that he would also crack open his sister's head if he kicked them both out of the top bunk. As he told me about this memory, he would cry. "I am such a coward," he would say.

He was skeptical, but agreed to try going back to the womb when I suggested it might be helpful to do that. We established "yes," "no," and "I don't know or I don't want to tell you" ideomotor finger signals. Soon he was back in the womb, and progressed through birth somewhat uneventfully. His first moments in the delivery room were quite normal. His mother was awake and accepted him with some real signs of welcome.

I asked him to go back into the womb, which he did quite readily. I said, "Go back to a point where you know something important about your life." In response to this direction, he suddenly found himself out of the body and above it, looking down at his mother from a great distance, perhaps a hundred miles above the earth. He said, "I can see my mother, and I can see the history of both my mother and father. It's like the DNA that goes back for hundreds of years. The strands of abuse and neglect are woven together. I know that somehow it is my job to break into that DNA and change it, to interrupt it so that my children and the next generation will not have to suffer the same kind of abuse that the previous generations had." When we finished the exercise, he was focused on this task. "I have to break this cycle," he said.

A few months after this experience he brought me this poem.

I KNOW THEM

I look down and see my chosen parents—
I know them.
And I see their parents
And I know them.
I see all of their parents
I know all of them.
Yet, none of them know me.
Or, will they?

Some of my favorite souvenirs are the pictures I now have of being the presiding minister at the wedding of Andrew's daughter, and of holding his first grandchild at the baptism. I am convinced that Andrew has learned how to break the system of abuse, and that his children and grandchildren will be free from the pain he felt from the generations of abuse which affected him. Spirituality is now the primary focus in Andrew's life, along with his children and grandchild.

CHOICES BEFORE CONCEPTION

Alan asked if I would help him regress back to the womb and earlier, if possible. He had a friend who had told him about this experience, and Alan was curious. So I taught him ideomotor signals, and he went back to the time of his birth. His delivery and first moments of life were quite normal and routine. I asked him to reenter the womb and go back to an earlier time.

Soon he was having an out-of-body memory, in space, with a Being of Light. He watched another soul approach the Being of Light, and "heard" the soul say to the Light, "If you let me live, I will devote the rest of my life to you." Alan was interested, and decided that if this soul went back to its body, Alan would like to have this person as his father, because he would like to live in a family where God was remembered and worshipped. He knew that many people forget God after they are born, and he wanted this father to be able to remind him. So Alan selected him to be his father.

But as the years went by, the father forgot his commitment, and Alan forgot too. They lived their lives without the memory of God. Alan remembers his father telling him that he was part of the invasion in the South Pacific during World War II, and went ashore with the landing troops at an island well defended by the Japanese. He was hit, and had said, "God, if you let me live, I will devote my life to you." Then he passed out. The medics put him with the dead bodies, but later somebody noticed that he was breathing.

Alan was born almost two years later. He believes that when his father was wounded, his prayer at that time was heard not only by God, but also by Alan who was with God at that time. Alan believes that he chose his father then, and that he did so in order for his father to help Alan remember God in this life. The near birth experience helped him reconnect with his spirituality, and also strengthened his relationship with his father.

GOD'S HEALING SENSE OF HUMOR

John came for counseling because his marriage was shaky. He entered my office visibly upset, and told me that neither he nor his wife liked the way they were relating to each other. Often he would feel as if he were a little boy and his wife was his mother, critical of him. We spent two sessions in traditional therapy, which surfaced his doubts about whether his mother really loved him or respected him as an adult.

During our third session together he decided to be regressed back to the time of his birth, to experience being with his mother during the first hours of life. He wanted to know whether or not she had welcomed him when he was born.

As he regressed back to the time of his birth, he reported that he had felt welcomed and loved by her. She held him warmly even in the delivery room, was clearly delighted to see him. This was a very pleasant experience for him, and he began to have loving thoughts about his mother.

He then decided to regress back to his earliest memory. When I suggested that he could go back into the womb and then regress to the earliest moment of his life, he went back in time until he experienced being just a little speck in the womb. Then he continued floating back still earlier, and found himself in the presence of a Bright Light which he realized was God. Then it seemed to him that the Light was with him now, in this room, not just as a memory, but as a present reality. He began to ask God questions about his life, and received meaningful answers that became a great help for him.

Just before the session was over he asked the Light, "Will you be with me forever, at least for the rest of my life?" God answered, "Just a minute, let me check my calendar!" John began to laugh. The tension he had brought to the session was gone, and he left my office smiling. He called me several weeks later to let me know that things had changed a lot since our session. His marriage was much better, and he felt more grown-up and loved. It was interesting for me that despite the fact that John did not engage in any marriage counseling—his wife never even came in with him for counseling—the near birth experience had a profound influence on him, helping him feel loved, and helping him feel better about his wife.

JOURNEY TO THE STARS

Nancy regressed to the womb and then to an earlier time, and found herself in the presence of God somewhere in the middle of the universe, looking at the stars and planet Earth, feeling freedom, joy, and love at a time just before entering her body at birth. She spent several minutes quietly enjoying and reflecting on this strongly emotional experience. She became aware of some of the limitations she had put on her life. She began to experience the freedom not just as a memory but also as a present event, and to experience the presence of God here and now.

A few weeks after this event she called to tell me that she had just seen a photograph of where she was during her near birth experience. It was one taken from outer space by one of our astronauts, showing a galaxy that she said was exactly where she was, that she could recognize the place precisely from having been there in the near birth experience.

As I listened to her description of being in space, with the stars, I was reminded of Carl Jung's vision when in 1944:

> It seemed to me that I was high up in space. Far below I saw the globe of the earth, bathed in a gloriously blue light. It was the deep blue sea and the continents. Far below my feet lay Ceylon, and in the distance ahead of me the subcontinent of India. My field of vision did not include the whole earth, but its global shape was plainly distinguishable and its outlines shone with a silvery gleam through that wonderful blue light. In many places the globe seemed colored, or spotted dark green like oxidized silver.[1]

It is interesting that Jung experienced this vision before the moonshot by NASA—yet his detailed description is almost exactly what NASA reported from the moon, and subsequently from other missions in space. It would appear that the near birth experience, and certain other states of consciousness provide us with access into sources of knowledge and insight that go beyond our everyday capacities. Moreover, there is some evidence that going back through the womb to our own beginnings also allows us to go back and revisit previous lifetimes. While the subject of previous lifetimes may be controversial, this kind of near birth experience often provides the person with insights into their present lives and how the past, even the very distant past, can affect us.

CHAPTER SEVEN

RETURN TO A PREVIOUS LIFE

I could well imagine that I might have lived in former centuries and there encountered questions I was not yet able to answer: that I had to be born again because I had not fulfilled the task that was given to me.

—C. G. Jung[1]

Sometimes when I ask people who have regressed to the womb to go back to the earliest time they can recall, they will go directly to an earlier life. They will clearly and succinctly describe very different lives than they are presently living. They will describe their personalities during that earlier time, what they wore, what they did in that lifetime, and even thoughts and feelings they had during that time. As different as these other lives may be for them, there is also a sense of continuity between the themes of these past lives and their present ones. Suddenly, they find that these previous lives shed new light on the struggles they are presently having in a relationship, a career, or in their own feelings about themselves.

Because of the continuum of certain themes between their present lives and their past lives, it is impossible to dismiss such vivid images and insights as only imagination. While we cannot prove the existence of past lives, it is impossible to refute that these *memories* frequently play an important part in the working out of our personal lives in the here and now. Will we ever be able to prove beyond a shadow of a doubt that memories of these past lives are real? Perhaps that is a less important question than to ask what light these memories may shed on the meaning and purpose of our present lives.

Because the reporting of past lives has come up so frequently in the near birth experiences I have witnessed and assisted, I am convinced that this phenomenon cannot be ignored. As Stanislav Grof, M.D., points out in his book *The Holotropic Mind*, "In the process of experiencing episodes from past lives, people often heal emotional and physical symptoms that they suffer from in their present lives."[2] How this process works, and its importance in the near birth experience, is best revealed by the stories of people who have benefited by this process.

JIM'S LIFE AS A BANDIT

Jim regressed to the womb, and when he was asked to go further back in time he flashed back to an earlier life in a cold wintry place that seemed like it might be Mongolia. He wore animal skins, with a hat or helmet shaped something like a buffalo head. He had long hair and a beard, and was the leader of a group of ruthless bandits. They roamed the countryside killing without mercy, looting, and raping. He never seemed able to satiate his appetites, and became more and more cruel in his pursuit of pleasure and power. Finally the people in the surrounding towns formed an army and hunted down his entire band. In the battle that followed, he was wounded and bleeding, an enemy sword having struck a major blood vessel. He fell on his back, and one of the soldiers picked up a huge rock and crashed it down on his chest, killing him.

He remembers being grateful that he could die. Accumulating things, possessing women, killing those who stood in his way—these were such shallow and unfulfilling ways of living. He remembers being jealous of people who were happy in that previous life, because he was so unhappy. He seemed to live on adrenaline, addicted to the *high* it brought him, but always obsessed with getting more. Enough was never enough. He was always driven, always angry, always unhappy.

The memory of this earlier life confronted him with a theme he had trouble dealing with in his present life. Even when he knew that he had enough, he seemed always driven to accumulate more. The memory of the earlier life reinforced for him the desire to lead a loving life this time and to resist temptations to go for more wealth and power instead of love. The memory of his previous life helped him tap into something deep, something important for every human being—the knowledge that love is ultimately more fulfilling than possessions and physical power, that the very essence of who we are demands love if we are to be fulfilled as a person.

For Jim the near birth experience was very helpful. It does not matter to him whether his memory of a previous life is a memory of an actual life, though he tends to think that it is. Even if the scenes were not of an actual previous life of his, the message presented to him was an important one: A selfish life is not a satisfying life.

As Jim reflected on his near birth experience, he began to articulate questions about the conservative theology of the church in which he was raised. He realized that in the previous life he had led a life of crime, murdering and raping and looting, disobeying the commandments of God not to steal, not to kill, and not to commit adultery. But rather than being sent to Hell, he is here again, and is now given a chance to reflect on that previous life.

As a result, he no longer thinks that a person who leads a life of crime or does wrong things will go to Hell forever. He believes now that a selfish life is its own Hell, but the soul is not stuck forever in that life. His desire to lead a loving life now is motivated not by fear of punishment in the afterlife, but to enjoy love and joy rather than repeat an unfulfilled life.

It is interesting how the power of the near birth experience is often found in the very fact that the events that are relived provide a new perspective about the nature of our own beliefs. We may have very strong beliefs which cause inner conflict, as in Jim's story above, and the near birth experience lets us see a larger vision that can free us from those conflicts. We have truths revealed that let us put old beliefs behind us in order that we might move forward to a new way of understanding what our lives are about.

* * *

It has been interesting for me to be with people, helping to facilitate the near birth experience, when they find themselves in a previous life situation that feels totally foreign to them. Then, within minutes, or sometimes hours, of coming back out of that near birth experience they see the significance of the events they've just relived in their present lives. Charlotte's case, which I relate below, illustrates this point in a way that is both colorful and insightful.

CHARLOTTE (SHO-NEE)

Charlotte regressed to the womb and reported, as an answer to my question, "Do you have an earlier memory?" that she was sitting in a teepee, dressed in animal skins that were warm and comforting, though scratchy. Her husband was stroking her hair, and she was nursing a young baby. Her six-year-old son was also with them in the teepee. She said her name was Sho-Nee.

She paused for a moment, and seemed filled with confusion and fear, and then she began to sob. I asked what was happening. She said, "They've killed my son!" She had shifted to a time when her husband and the other warriors were out hunting for food, and another tribe had attacked the camp. She described her panic when she heard the thundering sound of the galloping horses, and the shrieks of women and children mixed with the war cries of those who were attacking. She did not know where her son was! She picked up her baby and ran from the teepee, searching for her boy.

She found him by a bush, an arrow in his chest. She began to scream, and then was killed with a spear.

She was silent for a while. She was back in the present now, sobbing, overwhelmed with grief. "I have no idea where that came from!" she said. "I don't know anything about Indians!" Then she described what she had remembered.

After her death she had experienced rising above her body, looking down at the scene, feeling sad, separated from her husband, from her daughter (who survived the raid), and her son. She mentioned that it had been her belief, as Sho-Nee, that she had to sing the death chant for her husband in order for his soul to find peace, and she would not be able to do that because she was dead. According to Sho-Nee's belief, which was the belief of her tribe, her husband was condemned to wander forever, restless and unable to find peace because she could not fulfill her role.

But then she smiled. She said that the soul of her husband had joined her. She seemed very happy as she told me, "We were wrong. What we believed was not true! My husband's soul did find peace even if I was not there to sing the death chant for him!"

There were two significant changes in Charlotte's life after her near birth experience. The first is that she began to understand that a religious belief is not always correct. She began to live more in keeping with her own inner knowing, with her own experience. She reminds me now of a Sufi proverb: *She who tastes, knows.*

The second benefit for Charlotte is one she would never have anticipated. A few weeks after her near birth experience she called to tell me that she had been afflicted all her life with a phobia about needles and shots. She never would have a flu shot or any injections, because she was so terrified. But she had realized since her near birth experience that needles no longer affected her. She had gone for a flu shot and felt no fear or panic whatsoever. She believes that the needles were related to the spear that killed her in the previous life, and that somehow the regression had helped her deal with that issue.

There are many surprises in doing this work, both for the person who facilitates the near birth process and for the person experiencing it. In Maria's experience, which I relate below, it was not her own past life that opened up to her but that of her child. Her near birth experience gave her an insight into a remark her son had made. In the process, she radically changed her own views on abortion.

MARIA'S ABORTION

Maria regressed to her birth, which was a normal delivery, followed by a time in the delivery room when she was being brought to her mother's arms. Suddenly she spontaneously emerged from her regression, having remembered an emotional event that happened when she was twenty-eight years old, just a few years ago.

When her son was about three and a half years old, he had said to her, "Mommy, why didn't you let me stay the first time I came to be with you?"

She didn't know what he meant.

"You know, Mommy. When I was in your tummy the first time and you didn't let me stay!" Then she realized what he was talking about. She had had an abortion before she was married. She hadn't told anyone about that abortion, and there certainly was no way her three-and-a-half-year-old son could have known about it. But he was telling her that he remembered the experience of being aborted, and that he had chosen to come back a second time. He wanted her to be his mother. She feels very bonded to him, and believes that he did indeed twice choose her to be his mom.

Her abortion was something she had never dealt with emotionally, but here it was being presented for her to look at. On some deep level she had always thought it had been wrong to have the abortion. But she had also thought that the baby had died, not that it would have a chance to live again as her child. Now she didn't know what to think, except that a person is more than a body, and does not die when the body dies. She has always been interested in psychology and spirituality, and has now (in the year 2000) completed a master's degree in psychology.

She would have done this even if she had not experienced the near birth process, but the near birth experience did increase her awareness of her own spirituality and of the possibility of life before this life.

When she reflected on her experience with the near birth experience, she told me it had changed her mind about the issue of abortion. She had formerly thought that a feminist should be for abortion, that the right to choose was important. But now she thinks that it is the men who benefit from abortion, not the women. "They are the ones who get to play around without any responsibility. If we get an abortion, that puts the whole responsibility on women, and the men get off free!"

She thinks that the desire to convince women that abortion is a right they should fight for is a way for men to put the whole idea of birth control on women, and that is not fair. She has become a counselor, and plans to use the near birth experience as one of her tools to help other people. She has always felt close to her son, and the near birth experience has helped reinforce this bond.

The experience of a past life story may reveal a life purpose which the person was previously confused or unclear about. Even minor events, such as certain tastes we develop in our present life, or interests that attract us, are explained as we venture into our most distant memories. When these interests and tastes are explained through the near birth process, seeming indeed to confirm the previous life memory, the effect can be quite dramatic.

A HEALING BRIDGE IS BORN

Alois was a member of the faculty at a retreat center in Washington State when I was invited to demonstrate the use of the near birth experience. He was very interested in the near birth experience, and volunteered to regress back to the womb using this process. He easily regressed to the womb, and then spontaneously found himself in a previous life. He was fourteen years old, and was with a man in uniform who was saying in German, "You stupid Jew Swine!" Alois protested, in German, "Leave me in peace. I have done nothing wrong! What have I done?"

Even as he was protesting, the uniformed man took a pistol and shot him through the forehead, killing him. This was done before the Second World War started, and before the concentration camps were in existence, probably in the mid to late 1930s. Alois was not sure of the date, but that is what it seemed. In this life he was born in 1940.

Within a minute or so after being killed, the Alois of the previous life, whose name he did not remember, drifted above his body and then was in the presence of a Being of Light who told him that in his next life (this one) he would have the job of helping bridge the gap between Germans and Jews, and that the best way to do this would be to be born as a Jew in America and to go back to Germany to marry a woman whose family had been involved in the persecution of the Jews.

Alois was very excited about this session, for it explained some things in his life that, until then, had been puzzling to him. For instance, when his mother in this life was pregnant with him, in 1940, living in Wisconsin, she developed a strange craving for German beer. Until then, she had not liked beer at all, and being a Jew, she didn't have any great affinity for Germany. She knew that Jews in Germany at that time were being badly persecuted. But she craved German beer, until Alois was born. After his birth, she no longer liked beer at all.

When Alois was a teenager in this life, he developed a desire to learn German, and to go to Germany. He did both of these things, and was strongly attracted to visit one of the concentration camps. He knew that some of his parents' relatives had been killed in one of these camps. When he walked the grounds of the camp he picked up some of the earth, wondering if it had cremated bodies mixed in it. He smeared the earth onto the back of one of his hands in the form of a "J", and then wondered, "Why did I do that?" When riding in the train away from the camp, one of the other passengers noticed the "J," and very emotionally told Alois of its meaning, that the Jews were marked in this way during WWII in the concentration camps. Alois had no previous conscious knowledge of that.

The near birth experience explained many things for Alois, and gave him the sense that he has chosen a purpose in this life, one that he had unconsciously been living. He has been married for several years to a German woman whose family had persecuted the Jews during WWII, and has spent a lot of his life's energy finding ways to help reconcile Jews and the Germans who had persecuted them.

I believe that the near birth experience convinces us to look beyond the limits of consensual reality, that is, to look beyond what society or our peers tell us is true or untrue. I tend to agree with Stanislav Grof's statement, in his book *The Holotropic Mind*, that "our lives are not shaped only by the immediate environmental influences since the day of our birth but, of at least equal importance, they are shaped by ancestral, cultural, spiritual, and cosmic influences far beyond the scope of what we can perceive with our physical senses."[3]

This question about what is real and what is produced in our own minds often comes up for people as they go through the near birth process. Those questions can become a source of distress until we understand that there is a very different set of questions to ask. I think the best way to illustrate this point is to share a near birth experience I facilitated in which a woman at mid-life had a totally unexpected set of events leap to her mind.

A QUESTION OF AUTHENTICITY

I see a little girl standing on the porch, listening to her parents fighting. She is wearing a pink dress, and she has blond hair," she began. It was June of 1993, and the woman speaking was fifty years old that day. We were at a conference where I had demonstrated the near birth experience, and she had asked me to bring her back into the womb to help her relive her birth day. I was helping her do this, as a birthday present. Several of her friends had gathered. We were sitting in a circle. Two friends had brought tape recorders, and they taped the session.

With the help of ideomotor signals she regressed to the womb, and then through the birth process. She especially liked being in her mother's hospital room a few hours after the birth, listening as her father and mother talked about who she looked like; was she more like her mother's or her father's side of the family? Her father was wearing a tie, and looked so young! He had died about ten years before our session, and she was so glad to have a chance to see and hear him again. She smiled a lot as she reported this memory.

When I asked if she would like to go back to a still earlier time, she said yes. She reentered the womb, and went back toward the time of conception, to the earliest memory she had. Suddenly she flipped to a memory of being on the porch, a girl four years old. I asked her where this was. It was Cincinnati, Ohio, in the year 1939. The look on her face was that of amazement and disbelief. She had not yet been born in 1939, she had never been to Cincinnati, and the girl she was looking at was white. In this life she was black!

She was listening to people she knew to be her mother and father, arguing in the kitchen. And yet she knew that they were not her mother and father in this life, and she had never been in that kitchen. She said her name was Amanda. I asked what her Mom and Dad's names were, and she said Richard and Gail. When I asked her last name she paused for a minute and then said, "White."

She shifted to another scene. Or probably it is more accurate to say *the scene shifted*. She didn't seem to have any control over what she saw. She was now seven years old, riding in the back seat of the car. Her mother and father were in the front. She heard her mother say, "Richard, slow down!" But he said that he was the driver and he knew what he was doing. He was drunk. He sped up, and ran off the road, running into a tree. All three of them were immediately killed in the crash.

As she related this memory, she began to gasp for breath and to hold her neck with both hands as she tried to describe the death.

Then she relaxed. She found herself, as Amanda, floating above the car, and soon she was met by a Being of Light who told her that her next life (this one) would be happier. She said that this prediction has come true, that she is very happy in this life.

But after this experience, she became distressed. Where did these images come from? She had been taught that reincarnation was not real, but was part of a false religious belief. Was it real, or not? It was difficult for her to validate her own experience because outside authorities had already convinced her that they had the ability to define reality for her, and what she experienced was not real.

This is a very understandable predicament. I also wanted some verification. My first impulse was to settle the conflict by writing the Hamilton County Board of Health and the Bureau of Vital Statistics in Cincinnati to find out whether or not there was an accident which killed Amanda, Richard, and Gail White in the early 1940s. They wrote back that no, they had no such record. But when I called them, they indicated they had checked the records by reviewing the family name "White."

As I thought about that, I realized that probably the last name of this family was not "White," but that the first names of the family members might be valid. "Amanda," in this life, is black, and her name is not Amanda. I think she was so surprised that in the previous life she was white, that when I asked what her name was, the "White" appeared as part of her surprised state of mind in viewing herself as a white girl in that previous life. I plan to check this out. I need that kind of verification. So I will go myself to check the records by first names, looking for "Amanda," "Gail," and "Richard"—people with the same last names who were killed in an accident in the early 1940s in Cincinnati.

But I think we have to ask, "Is it the *literalness* of a report that we should be concerned about in such matters? Even though I am convinced that Amanda did in fact live and die as reported in her near birth experience, I don't believe that the benefit comes from validating the actual event. Rather, the value of remembering a previous life is in what the story has to tell us. It is like an allegorical story, the sort so often used for teaching religious concepts. It is for our soul. It does not matter so much whether or not it happened. It is about us, and it exists as part of the inner world that shapes who we are. It has something important to tell us, but its importance may not be found in its literal meaning.

CHAPTER EIGHT

BARBARA AND THE "A-TEAM"

A little girl in the second grade at a Catholic school raised her hand one day to ask if she could go to the bathroom. The nun said no, because yesterday she had taken too long and she couldn't do that again. When she went home the little girl ate a bar of Ivory soap. The next year she ate a lot of bars of soap, and she failed the second grade and had to take it over again. And she was careful not to drink anything so she would not have to use the bathroom during school.

Her name is Barbara. When she was forty-two years old she remembered why she ate the bars of soap. The day she took too long going to the bathroom had been blotted out of her memory, but suddenly she remembered. A priest had seen her in the hallway and told her she had to come with him. He took her into an empty classroom where he sexually abused her. The soap was her way of washing herself clean deep inside, to be 99 and 44/100 percent pure. That was the slogan of Ivory Soap at that time—99 and 44/100 percent pure. But regardless how many bars of soap she ate, she never felt quite clean. She thought that God was a monster to be feared because it happened in his school, at the hands of his priest, and she never felt safe in church. She never felt clean or worth being loved—until the near birth experience, which was part of her counseling.

When I first met Barbara she was suspicious of me. She had little trust of men, especially clergy. But she had a very close friend, Carol, who was already a member of a group I led for women who had been abused as children. Carol urged and coaxed and finally persuaded Barbara to join the group.

For the first two meetings she was more a spectator than a participant, and when she met with me for individual sessions she insisted that Carol come with her, to help her feel safe. But after a while she began to open up, to relax a bit. Soon she was talking as much as anyone else in the group, more than many others. She talked about her antagonism toward the Church:

"It's run by men," she said. "Not just the Pope and the Catholic Church, but all of them. To be a woman in the Church is like being in a huge pot, cooked alive by cannibals, with a lid on the pot so you can't escape, and men sitting on the lid, keeping you down."

At one of our meetings she expressed rage at all men and said she wanted to smash things, her fury so strong that only destruction and devastation would satisfy her. So the following week we brought stacks of old plates and other dishes to a nearby dump where Barbara and Carol hurled them against the rocks, both of them screaming with rage; eventually, released from their anger, they dissolved in laughter. That was a day we have talked about many times, each time with a smile or a chuckle.

I began to look forward to the group sessions. Usually everyone else had already arrived when, with laughter and radio blaring, Carol and Barbara arrived in Barbara's convertible. They often brought lattes for everyone. That was when I began indulging in that Seattle custom, at first just to be polite, and then because I enjoyed it.

As Barbara began to trust me, she started to open up about her childhood and her personal life. During one session she told me that she loved and respected her father but often felt "icky" when she was around him. She remembered a dream of him bringing a huge horse into her house, a horse so big it could not fit in. She didn't understand this dream, but found it anxiety-producing. So we explored her memory of the dream, and she had a flashback that caused her to scream and cry. She had an image of herself as a child twenty months old. Her mother was in the hospital giving birth to her baby brother when her father bathed Barbara, and then rubbed her with baby oil. She was relaxed. It felt good to be touched. But then she felt something between her legs. It was so big it wouldn't fit in, and he held her and she was dizzy and she hurt and she felt like she was falling, and it was icky and sticky and she wanted to go to sleep, to make it stop.

As a result of this dream Barbara came to believe that her sexual abuse did not begin with the priest, but with her father. She thought because of this trauma she might have been unconsciously sending signals since she was a baby, alerting other predators that she had been victimized, alerting them that she would still act like a victim and not fight back if molested. She began to understand why her first marriage was so abusive, and why she had so much trouble in her sexual relationship with her second husband whom she had just divorced.

Barbara had very mixed feelings about sex. The pleasure it could offer and the potential for it to be part of a loving relationship were subverted by her memories of being used and abused. She also had feelings of low self-esteem due to the difficulties she had in school, beginning with her trouble concentrating during the second grade, a problem related to her abuse. She had failed that grade and had been a grade behind her classmates until she graduated from high school. As a teenager and young adult she had bouts with alcohol, which increased her difficulties and decreased her self-esteem. She decided to use the near birth experience as a way to help her better understand and cope with life.

She had trouble at first with the ideomotor signals. I asked her to put her fingers on her knees and to think, "Yes. *Yes*. YES!" She was to ask her body to signal "yes" with one of her fingers, and she would know this would be the "yes" finger because it would let her know. It might begin to tingle, or to feel heavy, or to get warm or cold. It might become lighter than the others and feel easier to move. It might move without her even trying.

This bothered her. She said she didn't like the idea of not being in control. This is not uncommon for people who were abused as children, because what they perceive is that when they were not in control they were in trouble. But she gave it a try, and was surprised that one of her fingers, the right forefinger, moved. Next I asked her to think, "No. *No*. NO!" and to let one of her fingers become the "no" finger. It was the forefinger of her left hand. Next I asked her to select a finger that would mean, "I don't know," or "I don't want to tell you yet." It was the thumb of her left hand.

Then I asked her fingers to signal an answer to each of these questions: "Is it okay for Barbara to go back to being in the womb now?" "Is it safe for her to do this?" "Will you help provide her with helpful memories?" Her right forefinger moved after each question, so I asked her to imagine being in the womb. What would that be like? When she had an idea about that, I asked her to talk about it and to let her "yes" finger signal when she was no longer using imagination, but when the body or cellular memory was helping her. She said, "It's warm, and dark." No sooner had she said this than her right forefinger moved. We were there.

We proceeded to the birth, which was quite normal except that she said several times during the process: "I don't want to be here. I don't think my mother wants me here either. I don't like being touched by the walls" (of the vagina). When she felt her head come out into the light, she was disappointed that she couldn't turn back. She felt herself being taken to an incubator, and she had the strong impression she was not wanted. She said, "I don't like this. My mother doesn't like me. She is going to try to kill me!"

She then suddenly remembered in sharp detail a scene she had repressed until now. She was almost two years old. Her three-year-old brother and her mother were in her bedroom, and Barbara was in her crib. She saw her mother bringing a pillow down to her face, and suddenly it was hard for her to breathe. She felt faint, and then blacked out. As she was talking about this memory, she suddenly began to gasp for air and she almost fell out of her chair. After a minute or so she revived. She was very agitated.

She told me she believed that her mother had been aware, at least on some level, of the abuse going on in the family. (The father, an alcoholic, had sexually and physically abused not only Barbara, but also everyone else in the family, including Barbara's mother.) She thought that her mother's intended way of dealing with this abuse was to kill Barbara, Barbara's brother, and herself. It was probably the only way her mother knew to escape from an intolerable situation. Barbara heard the sound of a doorbell as she was blacking out, and she vaguely remembered her grandparents being there as she recovered consciousness.

I asked her to go back into the womb. We would go to an earlier time to perhaps discover something there that could help. She went back in time, and soon found herself in empty space. She realized that she was remembering an out-of-body experience of a time before entering the womb. I asked her to look around and to describe what she saw. She saw a Light, and I asked her to go to it. "It is God," she said. She was silent for a while. Then she said, "God doesn't love me. He's sending me to be born to parents who will try to kill me. I don't want to do this." She seemed distressed. So I asked her fingers to signal what we should do. I asked, "Should we stop now, and discontinue this until later?" The "no" finger moved. So I asked, "Is it okay for us to continue; will it be helpful even though it is distressing for Barbara to look at what is there?" The "yes" finger moved. I asked her to talk more with God about what was happening until she could better understand the meaning of this memory.

After a pause of perhaps two minutes she said, "My mother needs help, and God is showing me that I can help her. God thinks I should be born to this family to help my mother. I can bring her some of the Light. She is in such darkness. And I can help my sister too. She is in such pain." Soon she was more peaceful, and the "yes" finger moved strongly. She was silent for a while, and then said that God had promised to give her a special charisma that would help other people who were abused. They would listen to her, and she could help them. She had been wrong about not being loved by God. She didn't need to control all of her life. She could turn some of it over to God, who would help her.

She now had a different understanding of her life. She had been born into a family where she would be abused, but she had been given the strength to survive. She now believed that her reason for accepting her life was so that she could help many others. She started to cry, and tears streamed down her face for several minutes.

There are more things in heaven and earth, Horatio,
Than are dreamt of in your philosophy.
—*Hamlet, Act 1 Scene V.*

When she stopped crying Barbara talked of having always known, on some deep level, that other abused people would seek her out because they knew that she could help them. It was very meaningful to her to have God confirm that this was her life purpose. She was relieved to think that her suffering was not a sign of punishment or lack of God's love, but a way for her to bring Light into the darkness of other suffering people.

She resolved to contact her sister who lives in California and to continue being a support for her.

Most of the time thereafter, Barbara began to love herself. She still had problems, and sometimes woke up at night anxious about how she would handle them. But she invested her energy in a career she liked, and became a successful entrepreneur. Her life was no longer filled with depression and fear. She had hope. She made contact with a counseling office at the Catholic archdiocese to let them know what happened to her when she was in the second grade, and they agreed to pay for her counseling sessions with me. Her life changed for the better.

She was doing very well, had benefited from her near birth experience and from the group counseling sessions, and her life was on track. After three years of meeting in group therapy twice a month, and in monthly meetings individually with me, she graduated from therapy. During the next year she would sometimes call me just to let me know she was doing well, or she would stop by my office with a latte, to talk briefly about what she was doing.

Then one day she called, asking if she could come in. She was having severe headaches. During the past six weeks her vision had become so blurred that driving was dangerous for her, and she was so disoriented that Carol drove her to my office. This time there was no loud radio or laughter announcing that they had arrived. She appeared at my office in great physical pain, and in considerable emotional pain as well. She wondered if her headaches could be related to unfinished business regarding her childhood abuse. I told her that we could take a look at that possibility. But when she described the severity of the headaches and how they affected her vision and her ability to add and subtract numbers, I told her to get a physical exam in order to rule out organic causes before we could work on the psychological and emotional aspects.

She went for an MRI and CAT scan. The news was not good. They found two fast-growing tumors in her brain, one the size of a baseball and the other the size of a walnut. She was immediately scheduled for surgery, where surgeons removed much of the base-ball-size tumor but could not touch the smaller tumor deeper in her brain. Barbara then began radiation treatments combined with chemotherapy. Her hair fell out. She lost weight. But she began to feel better as the tumors shrank. Her headaches disappeared, her energy returned, and she and Carol took a trip to San Francisco to spend a weekend in Barbara's favorite place.

Then her headaches came back. The tumors had not been com-pletely removed and now they were growing again. She insisted that the doctors tell her how long she had left, and when they were reluc-tant to make a guess, she demanded. She always was one to face the truth, to confront whatever faced her. They said that their experience with her type of cancer led them to believe that she would live for probably six months.

The next five months were remarkable. Barbara at this time was divorced from her second husband, and had been living alone, in a house she owned. She was not able to care for herself after the surgery, while she was taking radiation and chemotherapy, so Carol asked Barbara to come live with her in a guest room. Barbara agreed.

For the next five months Barbara was circled in love. Friends descended like angels from Heaven. They came from Alcoholics Anonymous, where she had begun her recovery from addiction twelve years earlier. They came from the group I had led. They came from the neighborhood where Barbara had lived. Her sister came from California to be with her.

They formed what they called the "A-Team," a group of nine women who rotated in shifts so that there were at least two people from that team in the house with Barbara at all times, day and night. They became her nurses, her sisters, and her cooks. They read stories to her, read Bible verses to her, sang to her, listened to her, stroked her hair, held her hand, laughed with her, cried with her, got angry with her, loved her. They gave up days at their jobs, gave up nights to sleep beside her room, brought health foods and herbs and made vegetable juices for her. The whole house filled with love. I had never known anything like it.

One day when I stopped by to see how Barbara was doing, I expressed to some of the caregivers my amazement at how much they were giving her.

"You've got that wrong!" was their answer. They were the receivers, they said. Each of them told me a story of how Barbara had been the key to their own recovery. She had been there for them when they were tempted to return to alcohol or drugs, and had stayed with them through sleepless nights and tense days to see that they made it. She had known when to call, when to invite for coffee, when to be tough and when to be tender. They said things like, "What she did for me I could never repay." She had sensed when some of the abused women were seriously considering suicide, and had known when and how to interrupt that process. What they said amounted to this: "God has somehow given her a special gift to be able to help those who suffer, those who cannot make it on their own. When things get dark, she brings the Light. She has made all the difference."

During the last three days of Barbara's life the A-Team was with her the entire time, taking turns sitting at her bedside. One night three of them had visions of her walking in the hallways and appearing to each of them with a message of reassurance. They knew that she was in a coma in the bed during this time, but insist that her presence was real. They all sang hymns, sang love songs, songs such as "You Are My Sunshine." The atmosphere of love was so vibrant that I could feel it in the air whenever I visited. Barbara's personal things had been brought from her house and had been in the guest bedroom with her for months. They included photographs of her dog and of people she cared about. She had given her dog away to a friend when she realized she was dying and could no longer care for it. That was one of the events that nearly broke her heart.

On the wall of the bedroom was also a copy of the serenity

prayer: "God grant me the serenity to accept the things I cannot change, the courage to change the things I can, and the wisdom to know the difference." The A-Team kept a candle burning in the room, and it cast a light on the wall.

When she died, I was the minister for her memorial service. During the service her sister told how Barbara had been a life-saver for her during times of deep personal stress and pain, lifting her from depression and giving her the courage to go on. Members of the A-Team talked about her ability to speak the Truth in love, to confront strongly, but to always accept people for who they are. The memorial service was a moving testimony to Barbara's life. Carol had purchased a grave plot for her, and after the graveside service she stayed until the workers came to fill in the grave. Even after the grave was filled, Carol stayed until it began to rain. She said, "It seems like the whole world is crying, doesn't it?"

I thought of Barbara's near birth experience, when God had said that He would give her a special gift so she could be a help for others who suffered, if she would be willing to be born into a home where her father would be abusive. She would be a help for her sister, and for many others. I wondered, and still wonder, if that is what provided the meaning in her life—if her suffering was a way for her to be able to love others, and was a reason she was so surrounded by love, a love so very visible during her last months of life. I thought of the many people whose lives she had touched with the Light: the A-Team, her neighborhood, and me.

I thought of Victor Frankl and his statement that there are three ways to find meaning in life: love, work, and suffering.[1] I thought of Elie Wiesel and the deep suffering he endured,[2] and I wondered if his suffering was part of his greatness, part of the reason why he has touched so many lives, part of the reason for his courage and integrity. I remembered a statement which had impressed me many years ago, and I couldn't remember who said it: "I don't know of anyone who has grown or learned anything about the meaning of life unless suffering has somehow been a stimulus for the growth." I wondered if Barbara could have been such a bringer of Light if she had not also borne the pain.

This is not to say that I welcome suffering. If it were a choice, I would be first in line to return that gift for something else. Carol still feels the pain of Barbara's death, and for two years now has missed her. They were soul mates, and Carol feels that part of her soul is missing now. Barbara carried the Light for her, and the dark times seem darker now without Barbara. Once in a while Carol will go to the guest room in her home and lie down in the bed that was Barbara's, and will feel the pain, and the love, and the Light.

About a week before her death Barbara talked to me alone. She was alert and her pain was temporarily gone. She told me that she was sorry that she had to die, that life had been tough, but she had enjoyed so many things. She was sorry she had to leave soon, and she knew it would be hard for Carol to have her gone. She then was quiet for a while and her eyes filled with tears. Then she thanked me. "I'm ready to see God again," she said. I noticed that she said "again."

A week later she did.

The opportunity to participate in Barbara's life, and in her death, was a rare privilege. She offered me a glimpse into a world of suffering which included the fearful world of an abused child. But she also invited me into a world of love, love shared by others who had been abused, by others who had become a family for her as they all began to find meaning and healing in lives that had been broken.

I am not yet sure what to make of the experience of some of her friends who saw her walking the hallway when we all knew she was in a coma, unable to leave her bed. The A-Team all accepted it as reality. And there is something else that I still wonder about. It happened about a month after Barbara's first brain surgery.

She was in my office with Carol, and was very optimistic. "I think I'm going to beat this thing," she said. She was wearing a baseball cap to cover her bald head. Her energy level seemed high. And then, without any warning, an overhead neon light—the entire thing, a base holding the neon tubes, and everything—fell from the ceiling with a crash, just missing Barbara. If it had landed on her, it could have killed her. At that very second I said to myself, "I don't think she is going to make it." It seemed as if I were witnessing her world crashing in on her.

But after a few minutes of checking to see that we were all okay, she said, "See, that proves it. I come through close calls all the time, and I come out okay!"

When a group of men later repaired the light fixture and rehung it, they were amazed that it could have fallen. It was securely fastened with screws into the studs, and had held for many years, even through an earthquake that shook the building a few years earlier. I wondered, and still wonder, whether it was just a coincidence or was it some kind of omen, a message that Barbara's life was threatened and that she was not safe, that her cancer would shake her world or crash in on her.

Of course, we will never know. But I am beginning to accept events as real even if they cannot be proved through empirical means or the scientific method. C. G. Jung called them "synchronicities"— events that have no causal relationships, yet signal an important truth. The world of the spirit becomes increasingly real and immediate the more I experience this work. To a great extent my connection with people like Barbara and the A-Team has helped to confirm beliefs and experiences that challenge the beliefs of consensual reality.

CHAPTER NINE

THE LIGHT AND THE
VOICE ON THE RADIO

In the crucial matter of locating a sacred place on which to build a new temple, Mulla Nasrudin's advice was highly regarded. He would explore large areas of land, and then at an appropriate time and place would throw a stone. Wherever it landed, that is where the temple was built. Every temple constructed on such a place soon became a holy shrine attracting thousands of pilgrims. This result was attributed to the Mulla's ability to identify a sacred place suitable for a temple. However, when people honored him for his gift, he would only laugh.

"Mulla, why do you laugh?" his puzzled disciples would ask, until one day he confided his secret to them: "Those who honor me do not know that anywhere the stone lands, it will rest on a sacred place, for God dwells everywhere. Every place is holy!"

The near birth experience shares Mulla Nasrudin's secret that God dwells everywhere. Every place is sacred. There is certainly nothing wrong with honoring a place by building a temple and making pilgrimages to it, but even without the temple, every place is holy! By the same token, every person's body is the most important of all temples. Each body is a holy place where God dwells. Through the near birth experience we can make a pilgrimage to the center of this personal temple and experience the sacred. In my work with others I have seen this happen many times over. But I have also experienced it for myself.

For the first six months of guiding others through the near birth process, I saw, heard, and felt what others experienced as they reported memories of being with God before they came into this life. I noticed that these encounters with God often began as a memory of a time before birth, then the person would speak of a Light being present in the room, no longer a memory but an experience in present time. At this point people were able to talk with the Light and experience a response.

This process fascinated me. But I was also curious; were these experiences real? When people reported that they were with God, what was happening? What did that *feel* like? What impact would such an experience have on my life if I were able to make this pilgrimage? To satisfy my curiosity I turned to Aerial Long, a friend and a counselor who had been at the workshop in Menlo Park with Dr. Cheek in 1991 and had learned the near birth process then. I had worked with Aerial as a client of hers, and I knew she was primarily interested in helping people find their spiritual center. I trusted her with my own search.

We met for several sessions. In the first one Aerial helped me regress to the womb, and then back to a time before this life when I found myself floating above my mother's body. My connection with my mother seemed very strong, as though it might have existed for many lifetimes. I had the sense that I was choosing her to be my mother for this life. Then I had some important insights about the nature of my relationship with her, insights that seemed to come from memories of many lifetimes. These insights turned out to be helpful for me. I regret that the details are too private to share here, since they would intrude on my mother's privacy. Following that session, however, I have enjoyed a better understanding of my mother and our relationship has flourished during the past several years in a way that has been very rewarding for me.

While this regression session with Aerial was interesting and helpful, it felt similar to my earlier experiences of "guided imagery," a technique where we draw upon imagination to deal with difficult life issues. It was as if the imagery had come not from memory, but from my imagination. But I wasn't sure. Maybe it was memory, maybe not.

In a second session I viewed scenes from what seemed to be a previous life. These were very vivid, but were also very dream-like, well within range of what my imagination could have supplied. I saw myself being burned at the stake as a heretic in the sixteenth century. That makes sense to me in the same way that a vivid dream makes sense. After all, being one who had challenged convention more than once in my life, the heretic theme has not been exactly foreign to me. I know that dreams often present psychologically relevant themes in this way, themes that are symbolic but not memories of an actual experience.

During my years as a parish pastor there had been times when people accused me of straying from strict orthodoxy in my sermons. Once the bishop invited me to breakfast. Over a plate of scrambled eggs and toast at a Denny's restaurant he told me that a member of my congregation had contacted him about one of my sermons in which I indicated that I saw no reason for trying to convert a person whose spiritual life was already providing a connection with God. I had especially noted how much I was learning from some rabbis who were part of a Jewish–Christian Dialogue I attended regularly. I told the congregation that I would have considered it arrogant to think that the rabbis should convert to Christianity.

Both the bishop and the man who complained to him were concerned that such preaching compromised the work of evangelism. The bishop suggested that I should not be so liberal, especially in promoting the view that the "unbaptized" were not in need of conversion. He did not threaten me or suggest that I be burned at the stake as a heretic, but did suggest that I might consider rethinking my theology and that it would be wise to conform to the orthodox Lutheran doctrine. If I found that I could not abide by Lutheran doctrine, perhaps I should think about a ministry that did not involve preaching.

The meeting with the bishop reminded me of an earlier time in my life when I was confronted with the issue of heresy. It was when I decided to marry Gail. At that time I was a member of the Roman Catholic Church, and she was a Lutheran. We chose to marry in the Lutheran Church. In 1963 the Catholic Church taught that anyone baptized as a Catholic would be excommunicated as a heretic if they married outside of the Church. The pastor of my home parish forbade my parents and family to attend our wedding because to encourage us would be to condemn me to Hell. That was the teaching, and it was a very painful one for me and for Gail at that time.

So, the scenes from the age regression were a lot like a dream—vivid and relevant to my life but not necessarily a memory from a previous life. They could well have been images derived from my unconscious mind symbolizing the conflicts I had felt. The impressions were unforgettable, however. The smell of the smoke which choked me to unconsciousness and death before the flames reached my body, the size of the tremendous horses the men who arrested me were riding, my sense of submission to the authorities rather than fighting when I was arrested and executed.

All of these impressions, even the details of the brown stone buildings that lined the cobblestone streets of what seemed to be rural France, left indelible impressions on me. Even so I tended to think of them as creations of my unconscious mind rather than as a memory.

I left my meetings with Aerial feeling that something valuable had happened, but not convinced that age regression was real. Nothing had happened to convince me that the near birth experience actually helped a person encounter God. I still wondered whether people's reports of such encounters were just products of imagination or hallucination. But then I had a session with Aerial that changed all that.

Just as the session started, not yet even into the process of regression itself, I told Aerial that I wanted to meet God during this session. She agreed that that would be our goal. Then, as I looked around the room, I noticed a large plant growing beside Aerial's desk. I had noticed that plant many times before. But now it seemed to radiate heat waves, similar to those above the asphalt on a hot summer's day. I watched with fascination as the air melted in front of me. Then my right forefinger, which was my "yes" finger, began to twitch.

As I watched, a yellow light emerged, about the color of the full moon. It became brighter until it blazed as bright as the sun, but I could look at it directly without any discomfort, even with my eyes wide open. I was fully alert, and we had not used any form of guided imagery or hypnosis. In fact, the session had not really begun yet. I was not dreaming. This was happening, really happening! It was the most amazing thing I have ever experienced and as real as anything I have ever experienced. But what was it?

As I watched, the thought came: *my brother*. My brother Tom had recently had surgery for cancer in his neck. The thought became stronger. So I asked, "Are you my brother?" I didn't really think this Light was Tom, and I felt a bit awkward, as if I were on "Candid Camera," but the thought was so strong: *my brother*. So I decided to ask, out loud. The instant I felt myself make this decision, the Light responded by blazing intensely brighter. I took that for a "yes." But when I asked, "Do you mean Tom?" it became dim. No. How could this be? I have only one brother, Tom.

Then I suddenly heard the song, "Jesus our brother, kind and good, was humbly born in a stable rude." I didn't really *hear* the song as if it was being played or sung in the real, physical or material world, but I could hear it inside my head. Now I realized who this Light was. I was flooded with emotion, intensely overwhelmed by love, fear, sadness, relief, and joy. Tears began streaming down my cheeks.

I asked, "What would you have me do with my life? I want to know." He answered, "You want to *know* so many things, but I have come to *YES* everything." I realized this was a pun, an ambiguity about the words "know" and "no." I understood his statement to mean that knowledge was not the issue, but love, which affirms and accepts and says "yes" to what is. To "know" is often to "no" everyone who believes differently.

For a very brief time, perhaps less than two seconds, he appeared in human form as a young man dressed in a brown robe and sandals. I was impressed by how joyful he looked. Then he took the form of the Bright Light again. He said many things, including the statement that he had wanted to be with me in this direct relationship for a long time, and he was glad that I had finally opened my heart. I had been a Lutheran minister for almost twenty years and had no idea that I had not opened my heart, but what he said brought cleansing tears of sorrow, relief, and joy.

Following this encounter, I was emotionally drained, but also energized. I alternated between thinking, "I have just had an encounter with God!" to questioning how my experience could possibly be real. I believed in my heart or in some core part of me that this was truly the presence of God, and yet my intellect was very skeptical. Could this be just my imagination? Did I want this so badly that I had hallucinated? To answer this question I asked for proof that this was real, that it was truly happening.

He asked what could convince me if what I had just experienced could not. What could be more real than seeing him and talking with him? What could be more real than the deep feelings of my own heart, feelings stirred by this presence?

I had recently seen the movie *Oh God*, with John Denver and George Burns. In one of the scenes John Denver had asked God to prove that it was really He who was doing strange things, and wasn't all a trick from his friend Artie. God was talking to him on the radio, and said, "How about this?" and it started suddenly to rain in the car, but not outside. That convinced John. So I said, "Do something like that to let me know, and I promise I won't doubt you any more. Rain in the car, or talk to me on the radio. Otherwise I may begin to think I'm going crazy and that you are a hallucination."

As I left for home, it got dark. Rain clouds, big black ones, formed. It rains a lot in Seattle during the winter months, but dark clouds like these are unusual. When I got home the power went out. I lit a candle. When Gail got home and stepped into the bedroom to change her clothes, the power was still out. I brought the candle into the bedroom, and told her that I had experienced something very different that afternoon. I hesitated, and then said I believed I had experienced God, but I wasn't ready to talk about it yet. She looked at me kind of funny, but didn't say anything. That's when the power suddenly flicked on for about one second, and the radio in the bedroom called, "Jerry!"

I asked Gail if she had heard anything, and she replied, "The radio said, 'Jerry.' " She didn't think that was unusual, despite the fact that our radio was not on when the power went off. She thought maybe the announcer was talking about geriatrics or something and we just heard part of the word. To her it didn't mean anything. But it convinced me!

My life changed quite a bit at that moment. I began to believe on a new level, things I had always said I believed, and thought I believed, but really did not believe until I actually experienced them for myself. When other people had experienced the presence of God as part of the near birth experience, I had acted as if that were really happening, but to be perfectly honest, I had always doubted. I had always believed on some level that God could be present in this world, but I had never actually believed it could be like this. This experience brought a new understanding to my life: *God is God.* It is a simple statement, but if it is true, then it changes everything. And I began to experience it as true.

I would have to say that in the long term this has changed me for the better. But as I look back, I realize that for a while I acted strangely. I began to wear a cross around my neck, and often would touch it to remind me that God was present in this world. At times I would see auras around people. Especially if they were sitting next to a blank wall, I could see waves of light, sometimes like halos around their heads and shoulders. When I closed my eyes, even at night in a dark bedroom when I wanted to sleep, I would see a bright light inside my head. The light did not keep me awake, but was very reassuring.

It took me about six months to return to a state that I now think of as "normal." I learned not to talk about what I was thinking or experiencing, because I could sense that those conversations were not accomplishing anything. However, it was shortly after my encounter with the Light that I decided to begin writing this book.

LESSONS FROM THE PAST

The near birth experience continues to be a major focus in my life, just as it has been for many years now, and I continue to study both its implications and how it relates to experiences reported by others through the millennia. Throughout philosophy and theology, both ancient and contemporary, scholars have spoken of other realities, ones we do not perceive with our everyday senses but which nevertheless have an impact on our lives. Celtic Christianity, for instance, has a concept of "thin spaces" which allow a crossing from the reality of the physical world into the reality of a spiritual realm. I think that is what the near birth experience does. It brings us to those thin spaces—spaces that allow us to cross into long-forgotten memories or into the realm of the unconscious—spaces which lead us to the very core of our being at the center of self.

The experience of the presence of God was the most powerful part of the near birth experience for me, but every aspect has provided value. My experience or memory of being burned at the stake for heresy helped me come to grips with my fear of saying things in this life that do not fall within the box of the Church's orthodox teachings. I think that without experiencing those memories I might have been afraid to write this book, for some of what I have written is anything but orthodox.

And as I viewed the scenes of my regression back to the sixteenth century something else happened. I became angry at my passiveness during that lifetime. I went quietly when the authorities arrested me and led me to the stake where I was executed. As a result of this memory, I vowed to have a voice in this life, even if others do not always accept my reality as true. This is a free country; each of us has a right to be ourselves, and to share what is true for us. Clearly, this theme is an important one for me in this life.

I also realize how helpful it was to see myself choosing my family for this life and recognizing the strength of my connection with my mother. Some of the difficulties we had when I was a young adult became much easier to understand and resolve, for I somehow knew what it was she was thinking and feeling as I watched her from above, before I came into her body as a fetus in this life.[1]

One of the most beneficial aspects of the near birth experience is that it has helped me understand the power of encountering the sacred. I began to understand why groups of people in the Middle Ages would devote their lives and resources to building cathedrals, which often took several generations to build. Somebody, maybe many people, had experienced God, and wanted to do something to pay homage to that event and honor it. I could see why some societies thought that the sun was God and would worship it. They had seen the Light—a Light so much like the sun. I began to understand why the priest or shaman or spiritual leader was the principal healer or guide for early societies and why prophets such as Moses had the courage to confront people as powerful as Pharaoh. This kind of courage and conviction must have had its source through a direct experience of God.

As I reflect on my encounter with the Light, what impresses me is the message that God has come to " 'Yes' everything." To me this message means that our judgments about people are to be put aside. Love transcends right or wrong.

The memory of being with God before birth and the experience of the presence of God with us now, has fulfilled something I had been seeking since I was a young man. The near birth experience, for me and for others, is an experience of love, an experience of finding a meaning in life. It brings not only an inner sense of well-being, but also a courage to live our lives honoring what is true for our souls. It provides us with a context for the belief shared by Nelson Mandela in his inauguration, that

. . . we were born to manifest the glory of God that is within us. It's not just in some of us, it is in everyone.

CHAPTER TEN

THE CHEESE SANDWICH

During lunch break at work, Mulla Nasrudin was getting exasperated. Every time he opened his lunch box, it was a cheese sandwich. Day after day, week after week, it was the same—a cheese sandwich. Though he had liked this choice the first week or so, things had changed.

"I am getting sick and tired of this lousy cheese sandwich," complained the Mulla repeatedly. His co-workers gave him some advice: "Mulla, you don't have to suffer through a cheese sandwich over and over again. Tell your wife to make you something different. Be firm with her if you have to."

"But I'm not married," replied the Mulla. By now, puzzled and confused, his colleagues asked, "Then who makes your sandwiches?"

"Why, I do!" replied the Mulla.[1]

T he messages of the near birth experience are many. For most people, these messages are centered around a single theme—that the meaning of our lives is related to God, to love, and to our souls. We learn that everyone is of infinite value. Everyone has the same spark of Divinity; all are children of God. Another message is that if we have a conflict between money and God, we are to choose God. If we have a choice between forgiveness and resentment, we are to choose forgiveness. If there is a choice between body and soul, choose soul. But there is also a very practical aspect implied in all these teachings, and this is one that is illustrated in the Mulla Nasrudin story.

This story points out that since we all pack our own lunches, we should be able to change the menu. If we are the ones making choices about our lives, it should be easy to live as we want to live. Knowing the meaning of life, we can make the right choices that will allow us to enjoy comfortable and fulfilling lives.

If it were that easy, we would all be living exactly the lives we want, or think we want. There would be no need for further exploration, and no need for this book. But it is not that easy—even when we remember who we are—even when we remember being with God before this life. I recall the words of St. Paul[2]:

> I do not understand what I do. For what I want to do, I do not do, but what I hate I do.

This is the human dilemma, that often the needs of the body overwhelm the needs of the soul, even when we remember who we are. Whether we are a person on a diet confronted with chocolate, a parent who has run out of patience with a stubborn child, President Clinton tempted by a White House intern, or a soldier confronted by the enemy, body and soul are often in conflict. Sometimes we are so overwhelmed by the needs of the body that we are not free to make a choice to act in the way we want to, to be who we really are. We all have found ourselves at some point in our lives facing the same kind of dilemma faced by Mark in the following story. We act in a way that we later regret.

MARK AND THE BURGLAR

Mark and his wife went to a New Year's Eve party scheduled to last until after midnight. But at about 11:00 the burglar alarm at Mark's home was triggered. The company which had installed the security system for Mark called the police, and then called Mark on his cellular phone and told him what had happened. Apparently someone had entered his front door, they reported. They told him the police were on their way, and suggested that Mark and his wife stay away from the house until the police had a chance to investigate.

The party was at a home very close to Mark's house, so in spite of the security company's warnings, he and his wife decided to drive home and check out what was happening. When they got there, everything appeared normal, so they figured it was a false alarm. They did not know whether the police had been there and left, or whether the police had not yet arrived. They waited a minute, and then decided to check the front door. It was locked, which made them pretty certain that the call had been a false alarm. They went in, and then noticed that something seemed different, but they couldn't quite tell what it was.

As they entered the hallway leading to their bedroom, a man with a pistol suddenly came yelling and screaming out of their bedroom doorway. He pointed the pistol at Mark's head and shouted, "Get the————out of here or I'll blow your————head off!"

Mark was so stunned that he couldn't move. For a second or more, a time that seemed to last forever, Mark stood in the hallway, with a pistol pointed at his head, in the way of the burglar's retreat. The burglar apparently misinterpreted Mark's inability to move as a hostile behavior. He pulled the trigger.

Click.

At the same second as he heard the click and realized that the gun had misfired, Mark dove through a hall doorway leading to a separate bedroom. He pulled the door shut, locked it, and buried his head in the carpet, lying flat on the floor so if the burglar fired again the bullet would go over his head.

Then he remembered his wife, who had been right behind him and was now standing alone in the hallway with the intruder. He had left her "in harm's way," a phrase he had learned while in the military, a phrase which now shocked him into an awareness that he had deserted her, had failed in his duty, had fled the scene out of cowardice and left his wife with no one to protect her.

At the same time as this realization shocked him into action and he began to stand up and open the door, he heard his wife scream. The burglar pushed her aside and ran out the front door just as the police pulled into the driveway and arrested him. Mark and his wife were now safe, except for what had just happened to their marriage relationship.

Mark soon discovered that the gun was his own. He had always kept the unloaded gun in a drawer on one side of the bed and the ammunition clip in a drawer on the other. The burglar had found the gun, but apparently had been unaware that it was not loaded. The "click" had not been a misfire, but the sound of the firing pin hitting an empty chamber.

* * *

What happened to Mark could happen to anyone. Or, to be more precise, Mark's *response* to what happened is a response programmed into every human being. When we are in danger, our body's instincts for self-preservation take over. Our body seeks to avoid pain, to resist death, to survive. A mother may run into a burning building to rescue her baby, a soldier may throw himself on a hand grenade to save his comrades, but that requires an ability to overcome the body's first impulse—to survive.

This instinct for self-preservation is often in conflict with the soul. The body cares what happens to us, and seeks to avoid pain. It wants to survive as long as possible. But the soul is eternal and will survive this life. It cares not so much what happens to us, but *how we respond* to what happens to us. It wants to live in love, which is more important to the soul than avoiding pain or death.

Sometimes the soul and the body are in conflict even when the issue is not survival or pain. For example, the body views sex as a pleasurable experience, sometimes even as a need. A person may see someone who is sexually attractive, and the body's response is to desire a pleasurable sexual experience with that person.

But the soul takes other things into consideration. Love, for instance. Not just whether I love that sexually attractive person, but whether a sexual relationship with that person will hurt someone else, such as my spouse.

This can be a considerable conflict, and many novels and plays have been written about a person's dilemma when in this situation.

This conflict has also been the topic of newspaper headlines and other news media, usually focusing on the sexual behavior of celebrities or political figures who have chosen the body's pleasures instead of the soul's desires.[3]

This conflict between body and soul often involves money or sex, because the body is rewarded by both of them. They provide a better chance for survival, and the body's need is to survive. But the life of the spirit conflicts with these values. Spiritual leaders such as Jesus, Mohandas Gandhi, Mother Teresa, St. Francis of Assisi, Buddha, and others tend to renounce both money and sex, sometimes taking vows of poverty and chastity. "You cannot worship God and Mammon," says Jesus. This conflict is illustrated by the following story:

A SANTORINI SHOPKEEPER

The difficult choices between God and Mammon not only change individuals but also change entire societies. My wife Gail and I were reminded of this in 1988 when we went to Santorini, a beautiful Greek island to celebrate our twenty-fifth wedding anniversary. Thousands of years ago, the island had been covered with volcanic ash. Some have speculated that Santorini is the island referred to in legend as Atlantis. More recently the excavation of an ancient Minoan civilization under the layers of ash has brought an influx of tourists— enough to require the building of an airport.

One of my most vivid memories of our trip to Santorini is an evening we spent with a shopkeeper who talked to us about the seduction of money and things. We had come to his shop several times to look at some of the artwork he had for sale. His practice was to offer us a glass of wine and encourage us to browse for a while, taking our time to examine the merchandise. During our last evening on the island we bought a batik of an ancient mural called "The Fisherman." After closing time we sat and talked with the shopkeeper over first one and then another glass of wine as he told us of the changes which had occurred in Santorini during the last decade.

When he was a child, there were almost no tourists in Santorini. The people who lived on the island raised grapes, herded sheep, or were fishermen. All the neighbors knew each other. Life was simple and connected to nature. When the tourists started coming, many of his neighbors opened shops. So did he. They began to make more money than they ever believed possible and became wealthier than they could have ever dreamed. Now his twenty-three-year-old son flies regularly to Athens, and spends little time with his father. Almost all of the children leave the island when they grow up, headed into the world that seemed so far away when he was a child.

"It is a strange thing," the old shopkeeper said. "All of us agree that we liked our life better before the tourists came, but we are all making so much money it has trapped us. It is like a seduction or an addiction. People don't go to church very much any more. There are many churches on the island, but most of them are empty now. It used to be that the *Papas* (the Greek Orthodox Priest) was an important respected elder, and our values were about God and family. Now everything has changed."

He said this with obvious sadness. By the end of the evening he had indicated that he was drinking more wine now, enough to be a little high each night before he went to bed. He thought he was drinking more due to his unhappiness about the way things were going, that somehow he had sold out.

I think we all know what the shopkeeper meant. As long as body and soul co-exist, we will experience conflict, and there will be times when the voice of the body wins out over the voice of the soul. Like the Santorini shopkeeper, we will make choices that are determined by our desire to satisfy the needs of the body rather than to honor the soul. There will be times when we too will feel we have sold out, times when we will regret our behavior as much as Mark did when he left his wife in the hallway with the burglar waving a gun.

In light of these temptations and difficult choices, how does it help to know the message of the near birth experience? The same question might be asked about what good it does to read the Bible or any other book that promises answers to life's dilemmas. I think the answer has to do with *hope*. A little child has hope when he knows that Mom or Dad will be there when he gets home from kinder-garten, even when it may be hard to be away from home and struggling to learn things at school. The near birth experience tells us we are in much that same situation, and that we will one day return home from school. The near birth experience helps us remember that we are much more than a body, and that there are truths to be found beyond our physical needs and limitations.

The message of the near birth experience is that this life may be a struggle, but sometimes a struggle can be good for us. Some people choose to climb mountains not in spite of the fact that it is hard work, but because it is hard work. They like the challenge. In the same way, we made the choice to come here, and it was a heroic choice. The awareness of who we are can help make our choice a good one.

Mulla Nasrudin was one day asked by his disciple, "Mulla, where is the center of the universe?" With hardly a second's hesitation the Mulla replied, "The center of the universe is right here, exactly where I am standing." Not entirely satisfied, the disciple asked, "But Mulla, how do you know this to be true?"

"That's easy," the Mulla replied. "Just measure from one end of the universe to here, and then from the other end of the universe, and you will see that I am exactly at the center!"

Each of us is at the center of God's heart, the center of the mind of God. No one is further away from God than the heart of God. As we journey to the center of self, we reach that place where we encounter the presence and the love of God, and where our memories of God coexist with the knowledge that we are on our way home.

ENDNOTES

INTRODUCTION

[1] p. 98. See the annotated bibliography for more information about Dr. Cheek's book *Hypnosis: The Application of Ideomotor Techniques.*

[2] p. 195. For more information about David Chamberlain's book *Babies Remember Birth*, see the annotated bibliography. You may also be interested in Dr. Chamberlain's new book: *The Mind of Your Newborn Baby*, North Atlantic Books, 1998.

CHAPTER ONE

[1] Tom Clancy has created a hero, Jack Ryan, who offers a new and interesting perspective—a president willing to give his own life for those he serves.

CHAPTER TWO

[1] For more information about the research relating to regression to the womb, the books and articles listed in the bibliography under the heading "Near-Birth and Consciousness in the Womb" will be helpful, especially the books and articles by David Cheek, David Chamberlain, and J. Rhodes. A good beginning book is *The Mind of Your Newborn Baby*, by David Chamberlain, published by North Atlantic Books, 1998. Dr. Cheek's book *Hypnosis: The Application of Ideomotor Techniques* is excellent.

[2] In order not to influence this regression, Dr. Cheek checked his notes only after the session with the daughter.

[3] Dr. Cheek was well aware of this phenomenon, however. For more information, see Chapter Six.

[4] I use the present tense here to convey the sense of what happens in the near birth experience. A person typically reports not, "I *was* with God" or "I see myself when I *was* in the womb." The memory is rather reported as a present event, as if it is being relived rather than remembered.

[5] The near birth experience is not the only way to recover these memories. Hypnosis, meditation, re-birthing techniques, some drugs, and even some forms of massage also allow a person to retrieve those memories while in an altered state of consciousness.

[6] This quote first appeared in the writings of Marianne Williamson.

[7] *All I Really Need to Know I Learned in Kindergarten*, by Robert Fulghum. Published by Villard Books, New York, 1988.

CHAPTER THREE

[1] An excellent resource regarding this technique is *Traumatic Incident Reduction (TIR)*, written by Gerald D. French and Chrys J. Harris, part of *Innovations in Psychology Series*, edited by Charles R. Figley, published by CRC Press, Boca Raton, Florida, 1999.

[2] Bill Grace is his real name. He tells me that he does not care if people recognize him from this account.

CHAPTER FOUR

[1] Quoted in *Wisdom of the Idiots*, edited by Idries Shah. Published by The Octagon Press, London, 1989, p. 146.

[2] See especially John Bradshaw's book *Homecoming: Reclaiming and Championing Your Inner Child*, published by Bantam Books, New York, 1990.

[2] Neale Donald Walsch has written several books which offer loving messages that seem to me to come from the same inner place as John Bradshaw's *inner child*, or messages people receive from prayer, or from ideomotor signals as they go inward for wisdom and early memories. Walsch's series of three books called *Conversations with God* are well worth reading. The first is published by G.P. Putnam's Sons, New York, 1995.

CHAPTER FIVE

[1] This story was told to me by Ray Williams, an elder of the Stillaguamish Tribe in Washington State.

[2] For more information regarding TIR, see the book by French and Harris referred to in note 1, Chapter 3.

CHAPTER SIX

[1] Jung, Carl. *Memories, Dreams, Reflections.* Vintage Books, New York, 1965, pp. 289–290.

CHAPTER SEVEN

[1] C.G. Jung, *Memories, Dreams, Reflections, p. 318.*

[2] Stanislav Grof, with Hal Zina Bennett. *The Holotropic Mind.* HarperCollins, New York, 1992, p. 130.

[3] *Ibid.*, p. 84.

CHAPTER EIGHT

[1] Frankl, Victgor E. *Man's Search for Meaning*. Washington Square Press, New York, 1963.

[2] Wiesel, Elie. *Night*. Hill and Wang, New York, 1960.

CHAPTER NINE

[1] This statement does not accurately describe what seemed to be happening. It seemed not as if I were entering my mother's body, but that I was entering the body of the already formed fetus which was in my mother's body.

CHAPTER TEN

[1] This story was told to me by Jamal Rahman, a Sufi teacher and friend of mine in Seattle, Washington.

[2] In the seventh chapter of his letter to the Romans.

[3] Choosing the other way does not make headlines.

ANNOTATED BIBLIOGRAPHY

Chamberlain, D.B. *Babies Remember Birth: And Other Extraordinary Scientific Discoveries about the Mind and Personality of Your Newborn.* Los Angeles: Tarcher, 1988.

The beginning chapters of this book offer scientific facts about the baby before birth, and then near the end of the book Dr. Chamberlain introduces "non-ordinary" findings such as the presence of consciousness in the womb and evidence of memories of previous lives remembered by his patients. Dr. Chamberlain is well aware of the work of Dr. Cheek, who was one of those responsible for the development of the near birth experience, and Dr. Chamberlain's book is an interesting beginning for those unfamiliar with this field.

Cheek, David B., M.D. *Hypnosis: The Application of Ideomotor Techniques.* Needham Heights, Massachusetts: Allyn and Bacon, 1994.

Written primarily for professionals in the fields of mental health, medicine, and dentistry, this book is a culmination of fifty years of clinical practice by Dr. Cheek, an obstetrician. Dr. Cheek—together with his colleagues Leslie LeCron, a psychologist, and Milton Erickson, a psychiatrist—were responsible for developing the near birth experience. It is good background material for those interested in the pioneering work done by Dr. Cheek.

Chapter 11: Uncovering Methods; Chapter 12: Ideomotor Search Methods; Chapter 14: Fetal Perceptions—Maternal-Fetal Telepathy; and Chapter 20: Hypnosis in Obstetrics, are particularly interesting and relevant to the near birth experience.

Eadie, Betty J. *Embraced by the Light.* Placerville, CA: Gold Leaf Press, 1992.

This is one of the most widely-read books about the near death experience, indicating the existence of the soul after death. It is related in content to Raymond Moody's book, *Life After Life*, published in 1975 by Mockingbird Books, Inc, which was the first popular book regarding the near death experience, and to many others, including those by Melvin Morse who wrote about children's near death experiences. These books all are related to the near birth experience in that they talk of the existence of the soul outside the body.

Frankl, Victor E. *Man's Search For Meaning.* New York: Washington Square Press, Inc., 1963.

In this book Victor Frankl, a psychiatrist, tells of his life in a Nazi concentration camp, and of his search for meaning in the midst of suffering. He concludes that there are three primary ways people find meaning in life: love, work, and suffering. His findings are consistent with the reports of people during the near birth experience who claim to remember that they chose a life of suffering in order to find meaning and purpose in this life.

Grof, Stanislav, M.D., with Hal Zina Bennett. *The Holotropic Mind: The Three Levels of Human Consciousness and How They Shape Our Lives.* San Francisco: HarperCollins Publishers, 1993.

This book recounts the personal experiences and research of Dr. Grof and Dr. Hal Zina Bennett regarding the value of non-ordinary states of consciousness. The authors explain Holonomic thinking in science, thinking which challenges the Newtonian conception of how the universe works. Their experiences lead them to abandon the belief that "our minds could only provide us with the memories of events we had experienced first-hand in the period following our births." Pre-birth experiences can be even more important than the influences of experiences after birth, they suggest.

This book makes uses of the authors' wide range of knowledge in medicine and science. They suggest that the world be viewed as a thinking, conscious, living thing rather than a machine which came into being by chance. They indicate that our language misleads us when we name something, for a noun implies something static. But in fact everything, every *thing*, is constantly in motion—something which might better be suggested by a verb.

The Holotropic Mind presents a new way of seeing things, a vision that can prepare the reader for the spiritual viewpoint of the near birth experience.

Hallett, Elisabeth. *Soul Trek: Meeting Our Children on the Way to Birth.* Hamilton, MT: Light Hearts Publishing, 1995.

This is primarily a book of reports by parents indicating contact and communication with a child before its birth, sometimes before its conception. It is similar to the book by Sarah Hinze (see below), but more comprehensive, addressing the questions, "Do we come into our life from another existence? Do we have choice in the matter?"

Ms. Hallett offers 25 chapters and 327 pages of information, and clearly takes the energy to suggest various interpretations of the reports given. This book has the indication of a fair representation of many reports given by parents who claim contact with their child when he or she was yet unborn, and it is a great introduction to the near birth experience, offering illustrations of life before birth and the interaction of the unborn with his or her chosen parents.

Hinze, Sarah. *Coming From The Light: Spiritual Accounts of Life Before Life.* New York: Pocket Books, 1997.

"We are all eternal spirits who lived in a heavenly realm of light and beauty before coming to earth. *Coming from the Light* will teach you about our origin in life's eternal journey . . . "

The above quote by Betty J. Eadie, author of *Embraced By The Light*, describes this book by Sarah Hinze, with a forward by Paul Perry, a co-author of several books about the near death experience. Paul Perry writes that he received a call one day from Sarah Hinze, who asked him if the people who had near death experiences had mentioned seeing spirits waiting to be born. On reflection, he realized he had.

This book is primarily the reports of over thirty people who remembered themselves as spirits before conception, or who connected with the spirits of unborn babies before they were conceived, and the author indicates that these memories can be reconciled with near death experiences, with Christian beliefs, and with ancient philosophies. It is a good, and brief (180-page) introduction to the near birth experience.

Jung, C.G. *Memories, Dreams, Reflections*. (Recorded and edited by Aniela Jaffe, translated by Richard and Clara Winston.) New York: Vintage Books, 1965.

Along with many interesting thoughts and ideas, Carl Jung reports guidance by a disembodied spirit named Philemon, and also talks of his own near death experience. Jung's concept of the collective unconscious is one of the earliest suggestions made by a psychologist regarding the possibility of knowledge beyond the experience of this life and this body.

Neihardt, John G. (Flaming Rainbow). *Black Elk Speaks*. Lincoln, Nebraska: University of Nebraska Press, 1988.

I find this to be one of the most interesting books regarding our essence as people, from the thoughts of a Native American whose world was being take away by invaders who killed the buffalo, killed the Indians, and brought a new culture of materialism to the land.

Rosen, Jay Eliot, (ed.). *Experiencing the Soul: Before Birth, During Life, After Death*. Carlsbad, CA: Hay House, Inc., 1998.

Contributors to this book include the Dalai Lama, Elisabeth Kubler-Ross, Ram Dass, Stephen Levine, Raymond Moody, Gerald Jampolsky, and many others who are well-known authors and researchers regarding the soul.

Particularly interesting are the chapters in Part II: The Soul Before Birth. Harold Widdison gives an important introduction to the material contained in *The Near-Birth Experience* in Chapter 6, "The Emerging Field of Pre-Birth Experiences."

Walsch, Neale Donald. *Conversations with God: An Uncommon Dialogue, Book 1*. G. P. Putnam's Sons, New York, 1996.

This book, along with *Conversations with God: An Uncommon Dialogue, Book 2* and *Book 3*, introduces the possibility of a conversation with God. This lays a foundation for many of the conversations with God found in the near birth experience.

Whitton, Joel L. *Life Between Life*. Warner Books, New York, 1986.

The author states in the introduction that we have lived before in past lives and will likely live again in future lives—that our current life is but a small link in a long unbroken chain. Much of this book is about the time between lives, a time the Tibetans have called the *bardo*, and which this book refers to as the *interlife*. This book is an excellent introduction to the near birth experience.

I have listed in the next pages other books that can serve as a reference for the topics discussed in *The Near Birth Experience*. I hope you find this list useful.

FOR FURTHER READING

Bradshaw, John. *Homecoming: Reclaiming and Championing Your Inner Child*. New York: Bantam Books, Inc., 1990.

Campbell, Joseph. *Myths to Live by*. New York: Bantam Books, Inc., 1972.

———. *Primitive Mythology: The Masks of God*. New York: Penguin, 1976.

Campbell, Joseph & Moyers, Bill. *The Power of Myth*. (B.S. Flowers, ed.). New York: Doubleday, 1988

Dossey, Larry. *Healing Words: The Power of Prayer and the Practice of Medicine*, HarperSanFrancisco: A Division of HarperCollins Publishers, New York, 1993.

Eck, Diana. *Encountering God: A Spiritual Journey from Bozeman to Baanaras.* Boston: Beacon Press, 1993.

Evans-Wentz, W. Y. *The Tibetan Book of the Dead.* New York: Oxford University Press, 1960.

French, Gerald D., and Harris, Chrys J. *Traumatic Incident Reduction (TIR).* Boca Raton: CRC Press, 1999.

Freud, Sigmund. *The Future of an Illusion.* New York: Norton, 1975.

Gerbode, Frank. *Beyond Psychology: An Introduction to Metapsychology.* IRM Press, Menlo Park, CA, 1993.

Hillman, James. *The Soul's Code: In Search of Character and Calling.* Random House, New York, 1996.

Ingerman, Sandra. *Soul Retrieval: Mending the Fragmented Self.* San Francisco: HarperSanFrancisco, 1991.

James, William. *The Varieties of Religious Experience.* Cambridge, MA: Harvard University Press, 1985.

Jung, C.G. The Concept of the Collective Unconscious. In J. Campbell (ed.), *The Portable Jung* (p. 569). New York: Penguin Books. (Reprinted from *The Archetypes and the Collective Unconscious.* In R.F.C. Hull [ed. and trans.], *The Collected Works of Carl Jung,* [vol. 9, pars. 87–110].) Bollingen Series XX, Princeton: Princeton University Press. Original work published in 1936.

Kubler-Ross, Elisabeth. *On Death and Dying.* London: The MacMillan Co., 1969.

Kung, Hans. *Eternal Life?* Garden City, New York: Doubleday & Company, Inc., 1984.

Lankton, Stephen R. and Lankton, Carol H. *The Answer Within: A Clinical Framework of Ericksonian Hypnotherapy.* New York: Brunner/Mazel Publishers, 1983.

LeCron, Leslie M. *Techniques of Hypnotherapy.* New York: Julian Press, 1961.

LeShan, Lawrence. *Alternate Realities: The Search for the Full Human Being.* New York: M. Evans, 1976.

Levine, Stephen. *Who Dies?* Garden City, New York: Anchor Books, 1982.

Moore, Thomas. *Care of the Soul: A Guide for Cultivating Depth and Sacredness in Everyday Life.* New York: HarperCollins, 1992.

Morgan, Marlo. *Mutant Message Down Under.* New York, Harper Perennial, 1995.

Mother Teresa. *Words to Love by.* Notre Dame, Indiana: Ave Maria Press, 1983.

Morse, Melvin, M.D. and Perry, Paul. *Closer to the Light: Learning from the Near-Death Experiences of Children.* New York: Ivy Books, 1990.

————. *Transformed by the Light: The Powerful Effect of Near-Death Experiences on People's Lives.* New York: Villard, 1992.

————., with introduction by Betty J. Eadie. *Parting Visions: Uses and Meanings of Pre-death, Psychic and Spiritual Experiences.* New York: Villard Books, 1994.

Newton, Michael. *Journey of Souls.* St. Paul, Minnesota: Llewellyn Publications, 1998.

Parabola: Myth, Tradition, and the Search for Meaning, Birth and Rebirth.

Volume XXIII Number 4, November 1998.

Shah, Idries. *The Pleasantries of the Incredible Mulla Nasrudin.* New York: Penguin, 1968.

Shannon, James Patrick. *The Reluctant Dissenter.* New York: Crossroad, 1998.

Shroder, Tom. *Old Souls: The Scientific Evidence for Past Lives.* New York: Simon & Schuster, 1999.

Wiesel, Elie. *Night.* New York: Hill and Wang, 1960

BOOKS AND ARTICLES ABOUT NEAR DEATH

Coombs, P. *Life After Death.* Downers Grove, IL: Inter-Varsity Press, 1978.

Kubler-Ross, Elisabeth. *On Children and Death.* New York: Macmillan, 1983.

Lundahl, Craig R. (1992). Near-death visions of unborn children: Indications of a pre-earth life. *Journal of Near-Death Studies,* 11(2), 123–128.

Moody, Raymond A. & Perry, Paul. *The Light Beyond.* New York: Bantam, 1988.

———. (1980). The psychology of life after death. *American Psychologist,* 35(10), 911–931.

Wilkerson, Ralph. *Beyond and Back.* New York: Bantam Books, 1977.

Zaleski, Carol. *Otherworld Journeys: Accounts of Near-death Experience in Medieval and Modern Times.* New York: Oxford University Press, 1987.

REINCARNATION AND PAST LIVES

Evans-Wentz, W.Y. (ed.). *The Tibetan book of the dead or the after-death experiences on the bardo plane, according to Lama Kazi Dawa-Samdup's English rendering.* New York: Oxford University Press, 1960.

Goldberg, Bruce. *Past Lives, Future Lives.* New York: Ballantine Books, 1982.

Head, Joseph & Cranston, Sylvia L. (EDS.). *Reincarnation: An East-West Anthology* (5th ed.). Wheaton, IL: The Theosophical Publishing House, 1985.

Kastenbaum, Robert J.(ed.). *Between Life and Death.* New York: Springer, 1979.

Lenz, Frederick. *Lifetimes: True Accounts of Reincarnation.* New York: Ballantine, 1986.

Milbourne, Christopher. *Search for the Soul: An Insider's Report on the Continuing Quest by Psychics and Scientists for Evidence of Life After Death.* New York: Crowell, 1979.

Netherton, Morris & Shiffrin, Nancy. *Past Lives Therapy.* New York: Morrow, 1978.

Rieder, Marge. *Mission to Millboro.* Nevada City, CA: Blue Dolphin Publishing, 1993.

Rogo, D. Scott. *The Search for Yesterday: A Critical Examination of the Evidence for Reincarnation.* Englewood Cliffs, NJ: Prentice Hall, 1985.

Stevenson, Ian. *Twenty Cases Suggestive of Reincarnation* (rev. ed.).

Charlottesville, VA: University Press of Virginia, 1980.

―――. *Children Who Remember Previous Lives: A Question of Reincarnation.* Charlottesville, VA: University Press of Virginia.

TenDam, Hans. *Exploring Reincarnation.* London: Penguin, 1990.

Wambach, Helen. *Reliving Past Lives.* New York: Harper & Row, 1978.

―――. *Life Before Life.* New York: Bantam, 1981.

Winkler, Gershon. *The Soul of the Matter: A Psychological and Philosophical Study of the Jewish Perspective on the Odyssey of the Human Soul Before, During and After "Life".* New York: Judaica, 1982.

Woolger, Roger. *Other Lives, Other Selves: A Jungian Psychotherapist Discovers Past Lives.* New York: Bantam Books, 1988.

NEAR-BIRTH AND CONSCIOUSNESS IN THE WOMB

Chamberlain, David (1981). Birth recall in hypnosis. *Birth Psychology Bulletin*, 2(2), 14–18.

―――. (1980). Reliability of birth memories. Evidence from mother and child pairs in hypnosis. Presented 1980 at American Society of Clinical Hypnosis Convention. Published (1986). *Journal of the American Academy of Hypnoanalysis 1 (2)*, 88–98.

―――. The mind of the newborn: Increasing evidence of competence. In P. Fedor-Freybergh & M.L.V. Vogel (eds.), *Prenatal and Perinatal Psychology and Medicine: Encounter with the Unborn, a Comprehensive Survey of Research and Practice* (pp. 5–22). Park Ridge, NJ: Parthenon, 1988.

———— (1990). The expanding boundaries of memory. *Pre- and Peri-Natal Psychology Journal*, 4(3), 171–189.

Cheek, David. *Hypnosis: The Application of Ideomotor Techniques.* Des Moines, Ia: Longwood Division, Allyn & Bacon, 1994.

————. (1961). LeCron technique of prenatal sex determination for uncovering subconscious fear in obstetrical patients. *International Journal of Clinical and Experimental Hypnosis 9, 249–258.*

————. (1962). Areas of research into psychosomatic aspects of surgical tragedies now open through use of hypnosis and ideomotor questioning. *Western Journal of Surgery, Obstetrics and Gynecology 70, 137–142.*

————. (1956a). Emotional factors in persistent pain states. *American Journal of Clinical Hypnosis 8, 100–110.*

————. (1956b). Some newer understandings of dreams in relation to threatened abortion and premature labor. *Pacific Medicine and Surgery 73, 379–384.*

————. (1969). Significance of dreams in initiating premature labor. *American Journal of Clinical Hypnosis 12, 5–15.*

————. (1974). Sequential head and shoulder movements appearing with age regression to birth. *American Journal of Clinical Hypnosis 16, 261–266.*

————. Ideomotor questioning revealing an apparently valid traumatic experience prior to birth." *Australian Journal of Clinical & Experimental Hypnosis 8, 65–70.*

———. (1986). Prenatal and perinatal imprints: Apparent prenatal and consciousness as revealed by hypnosis." *Pre- and Peri-Natal Psychology* 1, No. 2 (winter), 97–110.

———. (1989). An indirect method of discovering primary traumatic experiences: Two case examples. *American Journal of Clinical Hypnosis* 32, No. 1, 38–47.

———. (1992). Are telepathy, clairvoyance and "hearing" possible in utero? Suggestive evidence as revealed during hypnotic age-regression studies of prenatal memory. *Pre and Peri-Natal Psychology Journal*, 7 (2),125–137, Winter 1992.

Gabrial, Michael. *Voices from the Womb.* Lower Lake, CA: Aslan, 1992.

Mehler, Jacques & Fox, Robin (EDS.). *Neonate Cognition: Beyond the Blooming Buzzing Confusion.* Hillsdale, NJ: Erlbaum, 1985.

Raikov, V.L. (1980). Age regression to infancy by adult subjects in deep hypnosis. *American Journal of Clinical Hypnosis* 22(3), 156–163.

Rank, Otto. *The Trauma of Birth.* New York: Harcourt Brace, 1929.

Restak, Richard M. *The Infant Mind.* Garden City, NY: Doubleday, 1986.

Rhodes, J. (1991 Fall). Report on research project: Interviews with 2½ to 3½ year old children regarding their memories of birth and the pre-natal period. *Pre & Peri-Natal Psychology Journal*, 6(1), 97–103.

Rossi, Ernest L. and Cheek, David B. *Mind-Body Therapy: Methods of Ideodynamic Healing in Hypnosis.* New York: W.W. Norton & Company, 1988.

Verny, Thomas & Kelly, John. *The Secret Life of the Unborn Child*. New York: Delacorte, 1982.

Jaynes, Julian. *The Origin of Consciousness in the Breakdown of the Bicameral Mind*. Boston: Houghton Mifflin, 1976.

Pietsch, Paul. *Shufflebrain: The Quest for the Hologramic Mind*. Boston: Houghton Mifflin, 1981.

Samples, R. Holonomic knowing. In Ken Wilber (ed.), *The Holographic Paradigm and Other Paradoxes* (pp. 121–124). Boulder: Shambhala, 1982.

HYPNOSIS

Bandler, Richard; Grinder, John; and DeLozier, Judith. *Patterns of the Hypnotic Techniques of Milton H. Erickson, M.D., Volumes 1 & 2*. Cupertino, CA: Meta Publications, Inc., 1977.

Erickson, Milton, and Ernest and Sheila Rossi. *Hypnotic Realities*. Manchester, N.H.: Irvington Publications, 1976.

Haley, Jay. *Uncommon Therapy*. New York: W.W. Norton & Co., 1986.

Lankton, Stephen R. and Lankton, Carol H. *The Answer Within: A Clinical Framework of Ericksonian Hypnotherapy*. New York: Brunner/Mazel Publishers, 1983.

Wolinsky, Stephen. *Trances People Live*. Ashley Falls, MA: Bramble Co., 1991.